.103759   HV
              5822
Brill   H4
              B75

The de-addiction process

Date Due

CHABOT
COLLEGE
LIBRARY

THE DE-ADDICTION PROCESS

THE DE-ADDICTION PROCESS

Studies in the De-Addiction of Confirmed Heroin Addicts

By

LEON BRILL

Associate Professor of Psychiatry
Addiction Sciences Division
University of Miami School of Medicine
and
Director
Regional Drug Education, Training and Resources Center
Miami, Florida
U.S. Office of Education

With a Foreword by

Carl D. Chambers, Ph.D.

Co-Director, Division of Addiction Sciences
Department of Psychiatry
University of Miami School of Medicine
Miami, Florida

CHARLES C THOMAS · PUBLISHER
Springfield · Illinois · U.S.A.

Published and Distributed Throughout the World by
CHARLES C THOMAS • PUBLISHER
BANNERSTONE HOUSE
301-327 East Lawrence Avenue, Springfield, Illinois, U.S.A.

© *1972, by* CHARLES C THOMAS • PUBLISHER
ISBN 0-398-02532-0
Library of Congress Catalog Card Number: 72-75910

With THOMAS BOOKS *careful attention is given to all details of manufacturing and design. It is the Publisher's desire to present books that are satisfactory as to their physical qualities and artistic possibilities and appropriate for their particular use.* THOMAS BOOKS *will be true to those laws of quality that assure a good name and good will.*

W-2
Printed in the United States of America

FOREWORD

This book is a detailed study of the processes by which a number of confirmed heroin addicts achieved abstinence and left the "addiction system." The author's "life cycle" model of narcotic addiction is used as a base for presenting a series of intensive case studies and additional survey questionnaire data to elucidate the parameters entering into some individuals' becoming narcotic addicts and, ultimately, ceasing their drug-taking behavior.

The intensive case studies trace the steps by which a variety of long-term addicts of varied ages and class, ethnic and geographical backgrounds "made it"—in most cases with the help of treatment modalities such as methadone maintenance, the narcotics antagonist cyclazocine, therapeutic communities such as Synanon, Phoenix House and Odyssey House, and religious approaches; though in other cases on their own, without benefit of any formal treatment program. The studies are rounded out by the description of an addict family—mother, father, son—who were helped through methadone stabilization.

The section on "Findings" summarizes identifiable psycho-social factors, conditioning and other reinforcements entering into a person's becoming an addict. The etiology is viewed as multifaceted and complex, comprising as it does the initial adaptive uses of heroin, which eventuate in physical addiction and the addict life-style and self-image. In the course of this discussion, a variety of typologies, including those of Chein, Cloward and Ohlin, Brotman, and Lindesmith are examined in light of the data presented here. Other constructs found in the literature such as "maturing out," "addiction-prone personality," "the search for euphoria," and the host of psychological and social factors commonly assumed to be etiological for drug addiction are scrutinized simultaneously.

The book next traces the de-addiction process through the

v

case studies and survey data, pointing up the increasing mal-adaptiveness and stresses and strains of the drug life, subsumed under such concepts as "the pushes and pulls of addiction" and "reaching rock bottom," which finally impel the addict to seek abstinence and find his way back to earlier goals and conventional living. A final "Afterword" assesses the treatment modalities currently available to heroin addicts and the effectiveness of each. It concludes with a description of the recently-emerged, younger multiple-drug users, who pose new problems for treatment and management. Suggestions are offered for the prevention and treatment of this "new breed" of poly-drug users.

The book should be of direct value to all workers in the drug abuse field; as well as professionals in medicine and the helping fields, and workers in public health, education, correction, law enforcement, and social service. It can serve as an excellent text for students of social problems, including social deviance, psychopathology and mental health, criminology, probation and parole, prevention, rehabilitation and treatment generally.

CARL D. CHAMBERS

ACKNOWLEDGMENTS

T HE "ACKNOWLEDGMENTS" SECTION of a book often serves to reinforce the understanding that many books are not truly the work of a single author, but rather represent collaborative efforts, past and present, which add up to the final published volume. This may be especially true where the study deals with a technical subject and is sponsored by a public agency such as the New York State Narcotic Addiction Control Commission.

The "de-addiction" or "ex-addict" study described in this book was one of a series of studies conducted by the Columbia Bureau of Applied Social Research (CBASR) between February 1968 and May 1970, under a contract with the Narcotic Addiction Control Commission. Dr. Theodore Caplow and Dr. Paul Lazarsfeld of the CBASR were the principal investigators and Dr. George Nash was the Project Director. Directors of some of the other studies were Dr. Robert Hill, who conducted the "Teenage Use" and "Block" studies and Mr. Dan Waldorf, who directed the "Institutionalized Addicts" study for NACC. The author would like to express his indebtedness to these individuals for their suggestions and contributions to the study. Drs. Nash and Hill and Mr. Waldorf and their staff—Misses Sally Howlett, Carole Grossman and Messrs. Bruce Johnson, Abraham Geliebter and others—helped plot the outlines of the study and were continuously helpful as the project got underway.

The "Ex-addict Study" itself was directed by the author with the assistance of Mr. John Langrod, who held the title of Assistant Director. It had been planned, initially, to select a sample of drug users known to authorities from some earlier program or survey since it was assumed this group would include ex-addicts otherwise difficult to locate. This proved in fact not to be feasible, except perhaps with an extremely high investment in terms of time and money. The next idea considered was to study an earlier group followed by the author for the U.S. Public Health

Service Hospital at Lexington between 1952 and 1962. Access to these files was no longer possible, however, and it was therefore necessary to fall back on existing New York programs which employed ex-addicts and could put us in touch with their "graduates."

Towards this end, a questionnaire of 50 open-ended questions covering such areas as life history, treatment and the reasons for discontinuing drug use was developed. Interviews were subsequently conducted with representatives from such community agencies as the Lower East Side Information Center, Synanon, Teen Challenge, the Damascus Christian Church, and cyclazocine and methadone maintenance programs, adding up to a total of 21 graduates. These interviews were supplemented by ten intensive personal interviews, some of them lasting six hours or more, or comprising several interviews. A few of the ex-addicts were known intimately either in treatment or by virtue of closer association in a related program so that additional details or analysis could be undertaken. Our thanks are extended to these agencies for their participation.

Because the author considers methadone maintenance a major treatment modality for long-term, "hard-core" narcotic addicts, it was decided to expand the study to include such patients despite the fact that it went beyond the bounds of the original proposal. A supplementary study of Harlem Hospital patients in New York City was therefore conducted between January and April 1969. One hundred and seventeen patients were seen in all, comprising two cohorts: all patients who had been in the Harlem Hospital program two years or longer and were willing to be interviewed, and all who had been in the program only a short time. The actual groups included 50 "old" patients, 53 "new" patients, i.e. under six months in the program; and others who were "in-between," ranging from six to 23 months. A few were located at Riker's Island. To supplement these interviews, field reports were completed, detailing the attitudes of staff and describing the methadone facility. These findings were summarized in the paper by Mr. Langrod and the author, listed in the Bibliography.

Our indebtedness is also acknowledged to the New York

State Narcotic Addiction Control Commission, which controls the data; and specifically to the Chairman, Howard Jones, and Dr. Harold Meiselas, Director of the Office of Program Planning and Research, who made all the data freely available to the author. The largest contributions were made by Mr. Langrod, and Dr. George Nash, who helped conduct the surveys and later collaborated with the author in preparing a preliminary paper entitled "The Dynamics of De-Addiction—A Pilot Study." The initial findings discussed in this earlier report have been elaborated in the present volume, and the data rounded out by the intensive case studies detailing the ex-addicts' gradual encapsulation in, and eventual disengagement from their addiction.

My special thanks and gratitude, finally, to my secretary, Mrs. Ann Davie, for her painstaking assistance in preparing and editing the manuscript through its various stages and "vicissitudes."

L.B.

CONTENTS

THE DE-ADDICTION PROCESS

I

INTRODUCTION

THE FOLLOWING STUDY, comprising ten intensive case studies (eight are included here) and twenty-one survey questionnaire interviews with ex-addicts, was planned with the aim of learning more about the factors contributing to the de-addiction process; i.e. the elements which helped some confirmed heroin addicts "make it" and leave the addiction system. It was anticipated that use of a "life cycle" model would serve to reveal in depth the continuous evolution of individuals to addiction and away from it, enhance our understanding of the intricate processes involved and, hopefully, offer perspective on the approaches required to help them grow out of their addiction as well.

Before discussing the methodology and rationale used for this study, it should be emphasized that the cases studied were selected and include a bias towards middle-class addicts and professional ex-addicts working in programs such as Phoenix House, Synanon, methadone maintenance, cyclazocine, the Pentacostal Church, as well as some not involved in any program at all. We shall touch on the common social and psychological problems and troubled family constellations observed, which appear to have contributed to their having become addicts and to have fostered a high tolerance for the "junkie" image and deviant way of life. Lest we see only negatives, however, every effort will be made to highlight the adaptive uses of drugs and concomitant addictive life style as well.

It will be helpful to examine these elements later in light of the typologies developed by Chein and Brotman and our own *life cycle concept;* and to check how our ex-addicts fit into these various typologies. In our exposition, each case study will follow the life cycle model promulgated by the author and colleagues several years ago. We shall also use as reference points such sociological theories as Merton's "status-frustration" hypothesis; Cloward and Ohlin's theories regarding "differential access" and addicts as "double losers" and "retreatists"; and Lindesmith's theory regarding the role played by recognition of withdrawal distress as *the* major factor in becoming an addict.[1-5]

In our discussion, care will be taken to stress the idiosyncratic factors which create an addict and ultimately help him grow out of the "addiction system." The author, in previous writings, has repeatedly stressed the belief that there is no one type of addict, but rather a variety of addicts from different class, ethnic and geographical backgrounds, and with varied ages and stages of addiction. We shall nevertheless attempt to determine what general elements in the etiology and subsequent life course of addiction can be extrapolated from the cases discussed; describe the psychosocial problems and family constellations which figured in these individuals' becoming addicts; and the sociological components which helped foster their initial high tolerance for deviancy and drug use and readiness to accept the junkie image and accompanying way of life.

Methodologically, the case studies were meant to supplement the larger survey and questionnaire interviews conducted earlier in the hope of adding depth and learning more about the parameters which helped some patients from selected treatment modalities, and others, who made it without the help of formal treatment, end their addiction.[6, 7] Toward this end, "graduates" of the Synanon, methadone maintenance, narcotics antagonist cyclazocine, and other approaches were interviewed as well as those who had passed through no major modality, but experienced the customary revolving door existence of hospitals, jail, and perhaps brief exposures to treatment of some kind without ever becoming more fully engaged, until their use became seriously maladaptive and they desperately began to seek a way out.

Though there are questions in presenting such cases, it must be assumed that what happened with these men must also have occurred with a very large number of other users; and this is indeed borne out by the author's experience wtih several thousands of addicts in a variety of follow-up studies, research, and demonstration programs as well as in individual and group therapy. It is obviously impossible to avoid injecting the biases and stereotypes occasioned by our own "trained incapacities." In all such discussions, the peculiar orientations of the writer soon become apparent; and it is important that he at least define them in advance so that the reader can be encouraged to make his own judgments and analyses.

A number of additional problems adhere to any study of addiction. One aspect frequently mentioned in the literature is that much of the data offered by addicts about their life history is conditioned by long years of drug use so that the original situation is camouflaged or distorted beyond accurate recall ("masking phenomenon"). Another is that many addicts often tell an interviewer what he wants to hear since they are manipulative and readily pick up cues. Still another is that the specific psychological and social problems elicited may have had little proven bearing on the drug addiction itself. From the standpoint of dynamic psychiatry, this would be rather difficult to conceive, however, especially if we view the person from a Gestalt standpoint; i.e. there is meaningfulness and continuity in any individual's character and behavior. Another problem is that we may offer psychological "reasons" when the real or more basic problems are physical or metabolic. Dole and Nyswander earlier postulated a "metabolic deficiency" or "metabolic lesion" theory, though this remains hypothetical and requires substantiation. It has nevertheless played a major role in the treatment philosophy or "mythology" of methadone maintenance programming.[8]

Still another problem in undertaking any study in depth is the existence of unconscious factors beyond the cognizance of the individual ex-addict unless he has engaged in extensive therapy which brought his private motivations to consciousness. Since the case studies were based on interviews rather than extended treatment, this study, in part, represents the perception of a small number of selected ex-addicts, of how they grew into, and out of the addiction system and the causal factors they assumed in both instances. The author's own participation included recording these perceptions and then undertaking an analysis of them in as great depth as possible, relating these findings to the larger numbers of addicts treated and known in other capacities and studies.

As indicated, an important assumption underlying the study is that there is no such universal as "the addict," but rather a variety of addicts for whom becoming an addict, and later growing out, represented very complicated interactions of influences and slow steps towards increasing involvement in the addiction system. It is hoped to elicit some of the factors which moved these individuals to drug use and later helped them abstain and to ascertain what there was about a particular treatment modality which made them receptive to its effects. In attempting to elucidate the very complicated processes entailed in becoming an addict, the author earlier undertook to spell out a "Life Cycle of Addiction" outlining a conceptual model for the "street junkie." This paper detailed such elements as prior personality and social situation, the numerous reinforcements along the way which first helped initiate experimentation and then maintained the drug user in his addiction, the role of differential association, conditioning as explained by Wikler, Lindesmith's concept of fear of withdrawal distress, and others. We finally have Martin's recent studies on "prolonged abstinence," i.e. that it may take as long as six months to overcome the effects of sustained drug (heroin-opiate) use.[9, 10]

To recap briefly then, the assumption from which we begin is that the processes through which an individual passes to become an addict or ex-addict are extremely complicated and can never be "simplistic," single, or uniform. They emanate, rather, from a variety of life experiences and happenings which predispose the individual to the addictive life style and the negative image and "hustling syndrome" that go with it. Since Freud, we accept as a truism the idea that behavior is always multi-faceted and overdetermined in human beings. In drug addiction, apart from the initial predisposing factors, a number of interstitial points occur when further decisions need to be made along the way. For example, in a number of studies presented here, the subjects early needed to choose between two worlds—the "square" and the deviant, or the "good" and the "bad." For all of them, there were very great incentives and rewards, secondary gains and adjustive, adaptive values in being "bad" rather than good. One boy felt he could never please his father no matter what he did. By the fifth grade, he had given up and decided he could gain more by being "cool" and hanging out with the bad boys than by being good.

We must distinguish those factors which helped initiate use from those which helped maintain it later, pushing the neophyte experimenters from one level to the next until they became fully enmeshed in the "addiction system." The initial factors might include such aspects as "emptiness" and "depression," or wishing to be accepted by an older group with higher prestige value in the neighborhood, or having problems around sex, or rebelling against parental values, or seeking to emulate negative role models. The ability to move on to full use was related to additional factors, such as the ability to accept the negative image of a junkie and the drug subculture and to engage in the deviant behavior—stealing and hustling—which goes with it. Drugs thus serve not only negative ends, but have many constructive uses in terms of helping individuals achieve ego mastery and a desired social image (frequently a deviant one such as a gangster or pimp), functioning as a social lubricant and means of resolving daily problems of living. It will be interesting to learn whether these elements are similar for addicts of such disparate ethnic, class, and cultural backgrounds as are presented here.

To focus the study more firmly, it will be important to define what constitutes an ex-addict—and even prior to this, an addict. Like Chein, the author believes that one of the central prerequisites for being a true addict is the existence of "craving," which is fed by the wide number of elements enumerated above and becomes so overwhelming and central that it eventually leads to loss of control and compulsive use without regard for the consequences. For the sterotyped "street junkie," this addiction entails the severing of ties with the "square" world and fairly total integration into all aspects of the addict street culture. The original life situation is exchanged for that of the drug world and junkie existence. "In the end, all reality resides in the needle." That this stereotype is not characteristic of all addicts may be evidenced by the author's studies of other addicts, such as the "hidden drug abusers" described in papers on cyclazocine and methadone,[11-13] some of which are described here. Though these addicts had used drugs for many years, they managed to maintain stable family relationships and well-paying careers and avoid being caught up fully in the addiction system. They were never identified as addicts and were never arrested or hospitalized; nor did they resort to illegal activities apart from their drug use.

Under our definition, the medical addict, the schizophrenic accidentally addicted, and the neonatal child of an addicted mother could not be classified as true addicts. To be an addict, one would need to have the craving and self-image, and develop the rituals, life style, and other accoutrements of the confirmed drug user. By the same token, to be classified an ex-addict, one could not use the measure of length of time abstinent alone since we know that many people may have been off as long as ten years or more, yet not have changed characterologically so that they are subject to relapse at any time. If they have been in jail or other institutions, they are likely to revert to drugs immediately upon leaving because nothing basic has been changed in their personality constellation. Or else, they may switch from heroin to other forms of drug abuse such as alcoholism. Wikler has described how addicts who have been institutionalized for years will develop "withdrawal symptoms" upon revisiting New York and viewing the George Washington Bridge. Since these symptoms could hardly be physical, they have been attributed to conditioning factors.[14] By this definition, too, mere abstinence alone cannot be considered a sufficient criterion of success or not being an addict. Additional criteria need to be brought into play, such as changes in life style and personal functioning, development of socially productive behavior, improvement in interpersonal relationships, reduction in criminality, better use of leisure time, and generally moving towards conventional "normal" goals and change in self-image.

While we have included methadone maintenance patients in this study, question may be raised since these individuals are still being maintained on drugs. Our decision to include them rests on the fact that methadone maintenance patients have changed their life style and are no longer functioning in the manner of addicts. Their being maintained on drugs approximates the maintenance of untold numbers of people today on various psychotropic drugs.

II

A CONCEPTUAL MODEL FOR THE LIFE CYCLE OF ADDICTION

THE GENERAL PROCEDURE to be followed in this study includes the presentation of individual cases, followed by analysis in depth in order to elicit the fuller meaning of each addict's initial and subsequent involvement with drugs and gradual ability to abstain. Following this, an attempt will be made to generalize the findings for the group of patients examined in order to learn in what ways a particular modality proved helpful to an addict. What emerges from our study is that, though a patient was often not aware of it, treatment he thought meaningless or even destructive at the time, such as a brief stay at a state hospital, later appeared to have been far more beneficial than he thought and to have had delayed effects which contributed to his eventual rehabilitation. By the same token, we shall observe that there are many smaller life experiences which may eventually crystallize into a total "push," which, together with the pull of treatment services, helps the addict find his way back to the real world (the "Pushes and Pulls of Addiction").

In presenting the individual case studies, we shall follow the outline presented in the author's earlier paper entitled "A Conceptual Model of the Life Cycle of Addiction." In this paper, the author and his co-workers outlined a paradigm describing the various stages through which an individual passes before he becomes a confirmed addict fully caught up in the "addiction system." This "Life Cycle of Addiction" is comprised of the phases which will be discussed in the following sections.

TOLERANCE FOR POTENTIAL ADDICTION

This stage includes the preexisting psychological and social factors which helped create an "addiction set," i.e. a high tolerance for drug use and the associated way of life, including the self-image of the junkie. Familial problems and social situation will figure prominently here.

Experimentation stage—irregular drug use. This stage includes experimentation with other drugs, pills and pot, sometimes liquor, culminating in a gradual, or sometimes rapid drift to heroin use. The most common course of this evolution is from "snorting," (sniffing) to skin-popping and ultimately to "mainlining," which involves acceptance of the self-image of the junkie.

Adaptational stage—regular use. This phase is characterized by the regular daily use of drugs in varying amounts. The addict is rapidly learning to relate his emotional and social needs to the world through the medium of drugs.

Physiological stage-addicted. In this stage, the addict becomes dependent on drugs, fears withdrawal symptoms, and develops the self-image of the addict. Most addicts proceed also to the life style of the street junkie, "hustling" and engaging in illegal activities to support their drug habits.

Tolerance of the addiction system. There are secondary gains inherent in being an addict since it may (1) provide an alternative type of status achievement within the deviant population and (2) place positive value upon a way of life generally condemned by society. The addict has a feeling of belonging and even feels superior to the square culture by being "hip" and "cool."

TRANSITION TO ABSTINENCE—TRANSITIONAL PHASES

Detoxification. The addict undergoes numerous detoxifications, though these serve little purpose but to bring him back to the social and psychological problems which impelled him to use drugs in the first place.

The addict seeks to escape from his addiction and self-image and substitute a new one. He shops around sporadically for various kinds of treatment which may help him make the transition back to abstinence.

Experimentation stage—building of tolerance for abstinence. A cycle occurs of addicts' undergoing detoxification, returning to drugs and again seeking detoxification as a kind of revolving-door experience.

Adaptational stage. The building of tolerance for abstinence through treatment. This can be achieved in various ways as through the use of such supports as a therapeutic community, chemotherapy, the "everlasting arms" of religion, probationary support and control, or personal relationships.

Tolerance for abstinence. The addict is emotionally and socially prepared to return to the normative community and function "normally." It is only at this stage that one can begin to talk of his being rehabilitated, "cured," and an "ex-addict."[9]

The "Life Cycle" paper suggests that the process of becoming "de-addicted" is as complicated as the process of becoming an addict. No one factor can be cited to explain why an individual changed and became an ex-addict. What seems clearer is that the addictive life gradually becomes as maladaptive as it was formerly adaptive in the adolescent period when the users were looking for kicks, rebelling, or else found that they could not cope with the problems confronting them and "copped out" through drug use. However, becoming an addict cannot be described simply in terms of "problem." We must also detail the many adaptive purposes served by drugs: as social lubricants; as one avenue for achieving for lower-class patients; as a way of identifying with deviant role models because they cannot do so with legitimate ones; and other factors described later under "Pushes and Pulls."

Our study did reveal that there were conflictual family constellations and social problems in all cases which contributed to the beginning drug use. This does not mean that all addicts necessarily start with psychological problems, or, if they do, that these problems are etiologic to the addiction history. We know that there are remarkably similar family constellations for addiction, alcoholism, schizophrenia, obesity, delinquency, and gastrointestinal illness, among others; and the family constellations described here could as readily have led to other illnesses. The "choice of neurosis" is a most complicated problem, requiring extensive analysis for its fuller elucidation. Obviously, also, if drugs were not available, these individuals would have found other means for solving their problems of living.

It is always difficult to generalize in case discussions since we can never lose sight of the discrete individual differences which vary from individual to individual. In the case of L.S. for example, the primary motif in his life was to test the love of his mother endlessly to learn whether she would stay with him no matter what he did; and this remained a factor to the end.

III

OTHER TYPOLOGIES

In ADDITION TO THE life cycle concept outlined earlier, use will be made of the typologies of Chein,[1] Brotman and Freedman,[2] and the concepts of Cloward and Ohlin.[4] A brief description of each follows.

CHEIN AND LIFE STYLES

An important recent innovation has been the effort to move away from psychiatric classifications alone and to study the person in his social milieu as well. With Chein, we get into more dynamic configurations since he intermingles psychological factors with four "life styles" for addicts:

1. Those totally involved, but without craving.
2. Those having craving, but not totally involved.
3. Those having both craving and total involvement.
4. Those with a history of repeated dependence without indication of total involvement or craving (the "situational addict").

These types obviously have different etiological backgrounds and prognoses and would pose different problems in treatment. Chein also postulates different uses for drugs: psychopharmacological for underlying problems, anxiety, and depression; and social uses including "situational use."[1]

BROTMAN AND FREEDMAN

Like Chein, workers at the New York Medical College have delineated four life styles though from a rather different stand-

14

point since addicts are rated on the basis of conventional behavior or criminal involvement:

1. "Conformists" are those who rate high in conventionality and low in criminality.
2. The "uninvolved" rate low in conventionality and in criminality.
3. The "two—worlders" are high in conventionality and in criminality.
4. The "hustlers" are low in conventionality and high in criminality.[2]

CLOWARD AND OHLIN

Chein's typology and further description of a "delinquent orientation" to life characterized by apathy and hopelessness correspond in many respects to other concepts such as alienation and "anomie." Merton, for example, indicated that when people are denied access to the goals society values, they may withdraw and retreat from these goals and have recourse to deviant substitute activities such as drug use. Cloward, building on this concept, further elaborated Merton's idea of "retreatist" behavior. Cloward agreed that when aspirations for middle-class status persist under conditions of limited opportunity or low expectations of achievement, pressures for delinquent behavior are experienced. These pressures are felt more acutely in the lower-class than elsewhere in the social structure. When criminal or conflict (bopping) behavior is not possible, the addict may resort to retreatist behavior under these circumstances. Drug addicts are "double failures" because they can resort neither to criminal behavior nor to violence to succeed. Cloward's theories have been criticized on the basis that they tend to stereotype all addicts and do not reflect their true situation.[4]

IV

METHODOLOGY FOR STUDY

GENERAL APPROACHES

To RECAPITULATE, THE book will describe the results of the first phase of a study of the career patterns of people who have stopped using heroin for at least a year and consider themselves to be ex-addicts. Although the total number of cases (thirty-one) is small and unrepresentative, enough has been learned from this phase of the study to warrant an investigation of the findings which have emerged. As part of the second phase of this study, 119 methadone maintenance patients who were formerly heroin addicts were also interviewed.[7]

Previous research in the area has largely attempted to evaluate the effectiveness of treatment programs for heroin addiction, or, more properly to see what proportion of those who completed various programs reverted to heroin addiction. O'Donnell summarized the results of a number of such studies which reveal that the proportion of persons who revert to heroin use is very high.[15] No follow-up studies have actually scrutinized the process of de-addiction, although several have examined factors associated with de-addiction by comparing those abstinent at the time of the study with those who relapsed. There is probably reason for this lack of examination of process. Heroin addicts come largely from lower-class and working-class backgrounds, and many are mobile. Some are very difficult respondents to locate in a follow-up study. Most of the effort of the study goes into locating respondents and determining whether or not they are using heroin, without considering other aspects of their life adjustment such as improvement in social productivity and interpersonal relationships, reduction of criminality, better use

16

of leisure time, and others. Little has been written about the process of de-addiction itself.

There have been three studies which, while not focusing specifically on the processes of de-addiction, nevertheless offer a number of suggestions for research. The first of these, by Charles Winick, led to the "maturing out" theory.[16] Winick used statistics of reported heroin addicts listed with the Federal Bureau of Narcotics, primarily individuals who had been reported by law enforcement and health agencies. When a person on the rolls of the Federal Narcotics Bureau did not come into contact with the authorities again within a period of five years, he was considered an "inactive addict" and removed from the rolls. Winick focused on those inactive addicts and discovered two things: (1) they had a median age of becoming inactive at about thirty; and (2) the overwhelming majority reported that they had been addicted to heroin less than ten years. Winick had no way of knowing whether these people actually stopped using heroin, died (the mortality rate is quite high), were institutionalized (many heroin addicts are institutionalized for large portions of their lives), or were simply undetected though still using heroin. Although his information was sparse, the figures suggest both a maturing out age and specific length of addiction.

Duvall, Locke, and Brill followed up dischargees from the Lexington Hospital with New York City addresses five years after their release from the hospital.[17] They learned that most people went back to using drugs soon after release from the hospital. Still, with the passage of time, more and more became abstinent. For example, of 40 white males who were voluntary first admissions to Lexington Hospital and under the age of thirty, 73 percent were using heroin six months after discharge and only 8 percent were voluntarily abstinent. However, five years after they had been discharged, only 34 percent were still using heroin, and 32 percent were voluntarily abstinent. (In each case, the remainder was institutionalized or otherwise involuntarily abstinent.) What this suggests is that people do give up heroin addiction even though they tend to revert after treatment; and studies which simply measure whether or not a

person ever uses heroin after treatment are bound to underestimate the results of treatment programs.[17]

A third study which helps round out the picture was done by
Robbins and Murphy.[18] They surveyed a sample of all black
men in St. Louis who had attended public school in the sixth
grade in that city. They selected a sample of men who had
attended sixth grade and were at that time between the ages
of thirty and thirty-five. Twelve percent of the men reported
that they had been addicted to heroin. (This is probably an
underestimate because some of those who became heroin addicts
probably died in the intervening years). Of those who became
heroin addicts, only 50 percent were still using some drug
between the ages of thirty and thirty-five, and only 18 percent
were still using heroin. This demonstrates that a substantial
number of heroin addicts do stop using heroin, with many giving
up all drugs. An interesting additional finding of the Robbins
and Murphy study was that all the heroin addicts in the sample
were known to the authorities, which suggests that in St. Louis,
at least, there is relatively little hidden heroin addiction. Unfortunately, the Robbins and Murphy study did not inquire at
what age heroin addicts started or stopped using, or how or why
they stopped using.[18]

SPECIFIC PROCEDURES

It was originally intended to focus on a group of heroin
users who were known to the authorities at a given point in time,
then to find out what proportion stopped using, when, and why.
It was also planned to compare users with non-users. So much
effort would be spent in locating respondents and securing
cooperation that we would not be able to complete the type
of lengthy interview desired. Most of the cases reported on
here were located through treatment facilities which gave us the
names of successful ex-addicts.

Two different types of interviews were conducted: in-depth
case studies of eight people were conducted by a clinical
psychologist. These interviews averaged at least three hours
each. Interview schedules were administered to twenty-one

respondents. These interviews averaged about an hour each. Two additional respondents were interviewed both in depth and through a questionnaire so that the total number of respondents equals thirty-one. Because of limitations of space, only eight of these studies were included here, with the precaution of having each modality represented, as well as two studies of addicts who made it without the help of any formal program.

Fourteen of the respondents were alumni of different treatment programs: five had been to Synanon or similar residential institutions, ten were from religious programs such as Teen Challenge and the Damascus Church, and eleven were enrolled in chemotherapy treatment programs (methadone maintenance and cyclazocine). Five of the respondents did not consider themselves alumni of specific programs, nor were they enrolled in any current program. Our ex-addict respondents were non-representative by virtue of the fact that most were located through specific rehabilitation programs. The majority were actually employed by agencies in the narcotics addiction field. Of the thirty-one respondents, twenty-three were thus employed in the addiction field and another 4 were seeking employment in the field. Only three were employed in non-addiction fields, and one was a houswife not currently employed.

Twenty-six of the ex-addicts were male and five were female. More of the ex-addicts were middle-class than is the case with the entire population of heroin addicts. Nine of the thirty-one were from middle-class backgrounds, thirteen from working-class and nine from lower-class backgrounds. Six of the thirty-one had completed at least some college, and another five had graduated from high school. Five more had acquired a high school equivalency diploma. Only fifteen of the thirty-one had not completed high school or the equivalent.

All thirty-one cases would be considered "true" heroin addicts. In addition, most were multiple drug users. All had used marijuana, and half had also used cocaine and barbiturates. Of the thirty for whom we have information, twenty-six had been arrested while using drugs, and only four had not been.

At the time of our interview, all had been off heroin for a

year or more and did not consider themselves in immediate danger of going back. At the time of our interview, the median length of time off heroin for our thirty-one respondents was 3.3 years. The range was from one to ten years. None reported that they were abusing alcohol or other drugs at the time of our interviews.

We have defined our respondents as ex-addicts on the basis of their abstaining from heroin for a year or more, their non-abuse of other drugs, and the fact that they did not perceive themselves as being in immediate danger of relapsing to drugs.

A number of other factors might be taken into account in building an index of ex-addiction. These factors would include at least the following:

1. Successful occupational adjustment.
2. Lack of criminal involvement.
3. Successful social adjustment.
4. Non-association with drug users.
5. Absence of other deviant behavior.
6. Change in self-image so that he no longer needs to consider himself an addict.

V

CASE STUDIES

RELIGIOUS APPROACHES
Case of Mr. C.

Tolerance for Addiction—Addiction Set—Predisposing
Familial and Social Factors

THIS PLEASANT-LOOKING, rather chubby, twenty-eight-year-old
man is a minister in the Pentecostal Church, and was articulate
though his image of himself is of an inarticulate person. He
seemed to have some block against the American culture since
he educated himself along the way at a theological seminary in
Puerto Rico and learned to read and write Spanish, but could
never do so in English. He is still having trouble and is
planning to take courses to correct his illiteracy in English.

Mr. C. began by saying he came to this country from Puerto
Rico when he was still a baby and lived in the "Barrio" at 110th
Street and Madison Avenue. This is a very rough neighborhood,
but his parents had no choice since they were quite poor at this
time. His father passed away when Mr. C. was ten years old
and life became doubly hard. He missed his father with whom
he had been rather close, and the mother spent all her time
working so that he had nobody around and little supervision
for most of the day. His mother paid another woman to take
care of him, but this was hardly adequate.

At the age of twelve, a crisis ensued when he learned that
these were not his real parents, but rather a maternal aunt and
her husband. This aunt had been unable to have children of
her own, and his natural parents surrendered him to her "even
before I was born." His father was a Nationalist in Puerto Rico,
and on the run all the time so that it was inconvenient for them

21

to have a child at this time. However, they subsequently had two children, but made no effort to get him, which he resented. He saw his aunt as his real mother when his real parents came from Puerto Rico and had to live with the aunt for a while. Later on, a psychiatrist suggested that he had felt abandoned and this might be a factor in his addiction, but he was not sure this was true.

Experimentation

At twelve, his hobby was flying pigeons on the roof. While there, he noticed that a lot of older boys who were back from Korea were busy smoking and doing other things on the roof, and he became very curious. He began to sniff Carbona with a friend and thought that all he wanted at this time was to be identified with some group and be accepted by them. In fact, he belonged to the junior auxilliary of a well-known gang-bopping group called the "Demons." At one point, he observed some of the heroin users stashing a load of bags, and he stole about one hundred and fifty of them since he was anxious to be one of the boys and to be a man. He plotted his strategy carefully, waited until he saw one of the addicts quite sick, and then approached him to make a deal: "If you teach me how to use the stuff, I'll give you some." The man agreed. Mr. C. was most anxious to learn what they found in heroin and to experience what they felt. The effects of Carbona had not been very satisfactory; in fact, they had been very bad since a friend died while using it; but Mr. C. was ready to do anything to get high and to be in a world of his own. He guessed now that he was "looking for Utopia or heaven and was also anxious to escape facing problems." He was also very miffed about the idea of his parents' giving him away when he was born, and he thought he must have been a bastard or at least unloved to have this happen. He had also begun using pot and liked it because it gave him a "social feeling."

He repeated that one of his guiding impulses was to be identified with the older heroin boys, to be part of, and accepted by them. The younger, auxiliary gang with which he was associating and which was primarily occupied with gang-bopping, warned him that he would become a junkie and he could then not be with them any longer. He therefore needed to make a choice, and it was unqualifiedly for the heroin gang.

After he made his "deal," the addict showed him how to sniff and he tried it, became sick and threw up. He stayed off a few days and then tried again; and this time, though a little sick, enjoyed the feeling. He snorted for a few months at the age of fourteen, but then found he was damaging his nostrils and asked one of the boys to show him how to skin-pop. By the age of fifteen, he was mainlining and was also pushing drugs. In fact, he was an emissary for some of the big-time connections since he could pass unnoticed because of his age. He was well rewarded for his efforts so that he never had a problem about copping drugs himself. At sixteen he began to be suspected of using and was arrested. When they did not find any stuff on him, he was held for unlawful entry. For the first time, while in jail, he became sick and realized, after somebody explained it to him, that he was hooked. He came out feeling sick and immediately tried to get high again. This time he was arrested again for possession and spent thirty days in jail where he kicked "cold turkey." He had dropped out of school at the age of sixteen.

Tolerance for Addiction—Adaptation

While in jail, an approach was made to him by a priest in prison. However, he felt the priest was a hypocrite since he carried a blackjack, and this disenchanted him. At the time, he was also rather disgusted with his aunt, who took him to a variety of spiritual places where they mixed religion with superstition, which he could not "buy." He spent some time now describing some of the meetings to which his aunt took him. They would sit around tables and say that there were evil spirits possessing a person and then try to exorcise the demons. This bothered him a great deal since he knew that there is a God and still believed in Him, but resented the superstitiousness and the "stupid voodoo" quality of the meetings. He was also concerned that some of the spiritualists were leeching off the parents and getting money from them for nothing. He was further annoyed because he had to bathe in certain kinds of

plant-herb preparations and rub certain ointments (Mr. C. mis-
pronounced the word as "annointments") or else carry a red
handkerchief and do other superstitious things he did not
subscribe to.

Also at this time, his natural mother became incensed with
him because his younger brother, who looked up to him, began
to follow in his footsteps by using drugs. This brother was the
"passion of my mother's life," the only one she really cared for
while she did not care at all for Mr. C. In fact, she behaved
quite destructively towards him. He was sent to Riverside
Hospital for the first time and saw a psychiatrist, but rebelled
against treatment because he felt "the psychiatrist was telling him
the truth" and he did not want to hear the truth at this time.
He simply laughed when the psychiatrist suggested he had
probably felt left out and was trying to fill his emptiness. He
realizes now that a lot of it was true, but it could not reach
him at the time. He also emphasized that he actually loved
drugs and would have liked nothing better than being high all
the time; but he was becoming uncomfortable with what drugs
led to and the things it made him do such as hustling, being
sick, and stealing. He was never comfortable with the junkie
image of himself: the entire reflection of the things associated
with drugs was "bad."

At this time, he entered into a strange association with his
natural mother. When he came out of jail, he learned she had
found that addicts were stashing heroin in her building, and she
appropriated the supply. Surprisingly, she gave it to him knowing
he was an addict, offering him the possibility of either using or
selling it. "This was the biggest shock of my life." He thought
his mother was using him to get money for herself, and he did
cooperate; but he asked himself why she would do such a thing.
His conclusion was that she did not have his welfare at heart
and was out to destroy him. He was hooked, nevertheless, and
came back regularly to the mother for drugs, which he either
used for himself or else sold for money. His mother entered into
a formal arrangement with the drug users, allowing them to use
the basement of the building if they gave her drugs in return;
and she continued this arrangement. By this time, the father

was divorced from the mother and she had remarried. She warned him not to tell his brother. She never offered the brother drugs, limiting it only to Mr. C. He concluded that the whole family must be sick and his was a "family problem." He felt the mother must have been angry with him from the very beginning because she gave him away to the aunt; and he resented this although why she should further displace her anger onto him was not clear. He felt his father had loved him and his aunt loved him, that everybody loved him, but his real mother, who took it out on him and never showed him anything but anger before he was born. He felt somewhat guilty after this outburst, added that the mother was a mere child herself when she gave birth to him and "things were different in Puerto Rico."

Tolerance for Abstinence

Mr. C. returned to the Riverside Hospital a number of times, and had greater freedom since the program was more experimental at that time, and they were trying to find out if somebody could be helped by staying only a month at a time. He therefore had free access to the hospital and used it merely to keep his habit within bounds, certainly not to get off. He was again arrested for possession of drugs and was sentenced to six months on Rikers Island. When he came out, he was twenty-two years old. He was fed up and tired; he knew he must find a way out although he did not know what it could be. He had been using continuously since thirteen and had been in fairly constant trouble. He was unhappy with the bad image of himself, especially when he saw others "pushing forward and making it" while he couldn't even read or write, a fact he was terribly ashamed of. He couldn't even fill out an application, so he had to settle for the worst jobs. At the age of twenty-two, he became desperate and decided to "pull a job." He was heavily hooked, had in fact lost control of himself and was mixing all kinds of drugs, combining heroin with bambitas, goof balls, and amphetamines. He especially liked the combination of Doridens,® or Seconals,® and heroin. His procedure was to take two Doridens, wait 3 minutes, then shoot up; and this made him feel the heroin more since it served as a booster. When he kicked, it was terrible since he experienced convulsions and bleeding from the rectum and was lucky to get off as easily as he did. He was very unhappy that nobody had seemed to care about his barbiturate addiction and that he was allowed to suffer. He had reached the stage where he was no longer just a heroin user or a heroin addict, but a "dope fiend" since he would take anything that came along and was completely out of control.

He heard about the Damascus Church and decided to walk in. He listened to the preacher and also saw his friend come over. This friend said "I am off and passed through this program. This place can help pull you through too." He agreed and slept in the church basement since there was no room and he was very sick. He was impressed by the fact that numerous members claimed they had been off five years and God had helped them make it. Since he came from a Catholic family, the junkie image had troubled him all along, and he found the new image appealing. In the past, he had resented the presence of statues in church, which he took as false images of God; but here he was in the actual Temple, and he cried not so much because of his illness, but because of his emptiness and his degrading experiences in prisons and basements. He demanded now that God prove Himself to him—he would like to meet and know Him. It had previously taken him about fifteen to thirty days, whether he was in a hospital or jail, to fall asleep. Now, after his challenge to God, he slept for the first time, and he took this as a miracle. Since that night, he has been off drugs.

The activities of the Damascus Christian Church engaged him totally at first since he went to their upstate camp and received religious instructions. He returned to New York and began participating in the church activities. After two and a half years of this kind of work and rehabilitating other addicts, he went to Puerto Rico to attend a theological seminary there. He had gotten the call to be a minister while in Puerto Rico and applied for the full course of study. He returned to New York and has since worked in various helping programs.

He was married several years ago and has had a wonderful marriage, has never been so happy before. As they say in the church, "free at last," and this is exactly how he feels. For some reason, the church represented a unique experience. In the Riverside Hospital, he didn't really have the feeling of ever being able to get off or even wanting to get off. For example, while there, he had tatooed "Born to Lose" in Chinese on his hand. He also showed me the word "Pachuco" which means "wise guy" or "troublemaker" tatooed. In elaborating what this "Pachuco" label meant, he explained that he had identified with the trouble-makers, and this was the image he wanted for himself. This was true from almost the beginning of his life, since when he first started to go to school, he had trouble with the tough boys and was labelled a momma's boy. He found out that he must join a group and fight back. In his neighborhood, this was part of the mores of survival in any case. His ideal image at that time was of being another Al Capone, and he loved the rough and tough existence which he found very exciting.

In 1952, after World War II, Spanish Harlem and a number of "social clubs" like the Dragons and Viceroys were being formed. He identified with these guys for protection; also he had too much free time in which nobody seemed to care what he did, and drugs seemed to be the only road open. He began going to school high and even nodding out, but the teachers did not seem to know what it was all about or even to care very much. When he said he was sick, they simply sent him home. He later felt the corruptness of many of the hospitals and institutions since he actually got more hooked in Riverside, so much stuff was floating around. This was also true in prison where he found the stuff circulating freely.

In regard to his other tattoo, "Born to lose," he had this done when he was over eighteen. He developed the complex that he was a junkie born to lose, and he wished to block out all the psychological problems he now realized he had. He fully expected to be a junkie the rest of his life and is still surprised that he was able to get off the stuff at a relatively early age. He is now twenty-eight and has been off a number of years, has no craving or yen, and would like to find a way of removing these tattoos as part of obliterating the past. His getting off was one of the greatest miracles in the world to him, and he relates it to the time when he challenged God to prove Himself. He now believes that it wasn't drugs which was his problem, but his inner emptiness which represented his isolation from God. He said that Christ is supposed to come to help sinners, and he was lost and needed Christ at this point. He realized through religion that junk had become as nothing to him; it was a thing of the past, and he now needed to deal with himself. Other kinds of treatment hadn't worked, although he would not want to close the door to them if they could help others. He himself, however, was fortunate in being able to go to Calvary, and Christ helped him make it. He is very happy with his new image as a minister of a congregation and with the respect he wins.

Mr. C. said there were no real men in his life except possibly his uncle. The crux of his problem seemed to be the two women, his mother and his aunt always fighting, and his being caught between them. Regarding his brother, he explained that he is still in bad shape. He tried to refer his brother to "Teen Challenge," but this didn't work for him. The brother has been seductive with him and tried to make him revert to drugs, but it has not worked.

As to Synanon, he was angry that they seemed to place their main emphasis on "insulting" and breaking down the boys' spirit. He thought this could never work for him and that it was a "lousy" approach. In discussing what he believed permitted the church in particular to help him, he felt it was the personal intervention of Pastor Rosado as a kind of father-figure who showed concern, cried with him, and at times even hit the boys to make them listen. He even followed users to basements where they were trying to cop, to stop their using drugs. He acted like a real father, something Mr. C. missed in his private life. He especially liked this intervention and the advice Father Rosado gave him. "I realized he was genuinely concerned about me and wanted me to follow the religious approach until I got off, and I did this."

In discussing any possibility of other personal problems as factors in his drug use, Mr. C. thought that sex had never been a hang-up, but education was his problem. For some reason, he had a block against learning to read and write in English, and this problem has continued, whereas he was able to do it in Spanish.

He admitted that he had loved junk dearly and is surprised now that this desire has passed. However, he disliked the junkie life and where it was leading him; he recalled that he weighed 99 pounds when he was converted. He had really hit rock bottom, didn't even have any shoes, his sneakers being worn through to the bottom. He was really a "greasy" type. One of the few gratifying things in his life was that his aunt always stood by him and always let him come home no matter what the situation. "She stood by me, and I love her. We always cared for each other." Interestingly, at first he said she was never married, but then explained that she was married but couldn't have children. Her husband passed away when Mr. C. was twelve as he indicated earlier. "He was like my real father and I have his name." Mr. C. dropped the remark that his father was an alcoholic. At home he was alright, but he did his drinking away mostly. "He was poor but good." He died by drinking wood alcohol, which finally "did it."

Mr. C. reiterated, "it was Christ that got me out of my trap. That day I was going to pull a job, pull a robbery, a burglary with tools, and if I was caught, I would have had a number of years in prison because I already had a record. Heaven extended its hand and I become a minister instead." In regard to religion, he thought that "man has his choice—either immortality to Heaven or Hell, and I chose Calvary. Man has a choice, a free will to serve God. Before that I was in bondage to drugs, and God delivered me from this. I accepted salvation; and, as part of this package, getting off drugs. My biggest problem since in religion, has been with smoking, and the difficulty was that I loved to smoke. It is ironic that after junk was no longer a problem, I was still coping with this, and I told God, 'You delivered me from junk, you can do it from cigarettes.' But God expects you to do something from your own will. In the church, I found a new spiritual birth; and I was reborn and had a new way of thinking and being." Mr. C. was concerned that his religious conversion not be misinterpreted as a crutch, when this was far from the case. Actually, this is a way of life with him now, and his salvation has given him an inner peace.

Surprisingly, he never O.D.'d, except one time he took four

Doridens and a shot of heroin and fell out. A friend woke him up. He said that three friends died in his own arms, but this did not help in any way to stop him.

CASE OF MR. C.   PENTECOSTAL

Brotman-Freedman Typology
  1. Normal conventionality   —
  2. Criminality and hustling   —
  3. Family conventionality   —
  4. Friend conventionality   —
  Characterization—"Hustler"

Chein Typology
  Drug use seemed to cover feelings of emptiness and depression, of being a "bastard" and unloved. He saw the mother as destructive and felt displaced by his brother.

Life Cycle
  Confirmed street addict.

Social Milieu
  From Puerto Rico to New York

Cloward-Ohlin
  Their formulation doesn't seem a major factor.

EX-ADDICT-DIRECTED THERAPEUTIC COMMUNITIES

Case of Mr. I.R.

Addiction Set—Predisposing Social and Psychological Factors

I.R.'s first traumatic experiences occurred at the age of twelve years, near puberty and around the time of his confirmation, while he was actually playing hooky. At this time, he was constantly incensed with his mother and father because they were an "inadequate family" who gave no love. He had a hostile interaction with the mother, who saw him as a threat since he was the apple of the father's eye. According to I.R., the father was a "psychopath" and kind of an Italian "Damon Runyon character," heavily engaged in underworld activities, counterfeit money, armed robberies, gambling, and excessive drinking, "although not a complete alcoholic." He also operated as a "skip tracer," which he explained as a con or "Murphy" man; and "shylocked" on the side. He was seldom home weekdays, but tried to be home on Sundays. He was a rather rough and brutal man, but "on the whole, he never hit me." He was a big-time spender who, when he came home, would give I.R. $100 and the mother $10. There were three children: an older brother, the "good boy" in the family; a younger sister; and I.R., who was the "black sheep."

Before puberty, I.D. was already engaged in stealing at the five-and-ten and playing hooky, but this was "mostly kid stuff." Two days before his confirmation, after all the relatives had been invited from far and wide to attend, he revealed the fact of his truancy. Between twelve and thirteen, he started his "alcoholism." His father's liquor was freely available around the house, and he had a great time mixing all kinds of concoctions. The year before the confirmation was a time of agitation, acting out, and trouble. He even fell in love with a girl "who rejected me; it was a heartbreaking experience."

Experimentation Stage—Irregular Use

Before age thirteen, the family moved to the Bronx. He got hooked up with the young "J.D.'s" in the area and began to pursue his "career," the only one around. There were still some conflicts between different directions since he had a friend, a "good boy" who was crippled, to whom he had been introduced by his mother. He began to hang out around the local garages and alleyways where there was plenty of pot to be had and was continually attracted to the older boys. The first time he used pot he felt nothing, but the second time he was "loaded out of my mind." He liked pot far better than whiskey, but for some reason continued drinking whiskey. He felt pot was hipper, quicker, and "cooler" than whiskey, which also left a bad taste.

He hung around the poolrooms, though he was underage, and saw dope circulating freely. He became involved with the older boys to the extent of holding the belts for them while they "took off." He was disconcerted when he noticed that some of the beginners threw up and had bad experiences. Before fourteen, he took his first shot and did it all by himself, injecting himself with part of a $3 bag and borrowing another boy's works to do it. He was now associated with a group that consisted half of Jewish and half of other ethnic groups—Italians and Spanish. When he got high, he didn't like the first reaction: he became sick, was frightened by the "rush" when his heart started pounding wildly, and began throwing up and dry heaving. This didn't prevent him from "taking off" six times more from the same bag of heroin, nor from snorting it with some of the guys as well, using only a tiny bit at a time. Interestingly, although he became sick, he also experienced a very pleasant reaction the following morning and was therefore tempted to repeat the experience. Though he was again frightened by the "rush" and the thought that he would die, it did not stop him.

Adaptational Stage—Regular Use

I.R. observed, "the rest is a blank," since it was hard to remember clearly what followed after his heart started to beat wildly. He was learning to combine drinking with drugs and pot. He was still attending school, fooling around, at first only every other weekend, then every weekend. He was associating with two distinct groups: one, the older boys he had mentioned; the other, a younger group of peers in which he figured as one of the leaders. For two years, he continued with his weekend use of reefers, alcohol and heroin, gradually slipping into the rest of the week until he discovered he had his first habit. He used it because it tuned him out from all the things he didn't want to experience, "especially my mother and father." The peer group became especially important because the whole thing "recreated" his family, since he was escaping and trying to be accepted, even to be a leader, and not to be compared invidiously with his good brother, cousins, or the downstairs kids. Through his acting-out behavior and anesthetization, he could block out all feelings. It was only long after he began therapy and had hospitalization that he could experience his feelings and realize what functions drugs had been serving.

As indicated, in the triangle between father, mother and son, the father preferred I.R. to the mother (according to I.R.) and helped cast him in a passive-feminine role. In terms of identification, I.R. emulated the sociopathic elements in the father; and the father, as an alcoholic or near-alcoholic, served as a model for his drug addiction as well. The combined destructiveness and negativism of the parents was focused on him in one direction from the father, and in another from the mother, who identified him with the father and vented her hatred of men and the father upon him. A "double-bind" situation resulted, with the parents unconsciously conveying messages that they expected him to act like a monster. This was confirmed when I.R. came home from Synanon later: he sensed the disappointment of his parents that he was doing well, which meant that they would need to re-arrange their own lives and not rely on his illness. I.R. grew up with a mistrust of authority and adults. There appeared to be elements of competitiveness with the father, in addition to a lack of sureness about himself as a man. At the age of twelve or thirteen, which was the transition year for him, he needed to choose between the image of a good boy or bad. His mother offered him the image of a good boy to emulate, but he rejected this to hang out with the bad boys. He already had a high tolerance for deviant behavior. He couldn't wait to grow up and achieve independence by associating with older boys. Interestingly, his first shot occurred on New Year's Eve, the point of transition to the new year. Drugs served many functions, including the blocking out of reality, especially feelings about his mother and father.

His craving was an unquenchable appetite which consisted largely of his search for oblivion, death wishes, and "tuning out." It also related to his inability to deal with reality; drugs became his means of putting himself in a glass cage so that he could be insulated against life. There was tremendous insecurity; he was unable to accept either uncomfortable or comfortable feelings, and he sabotaged whatever success he had.

He thus blocked out all feelings, and for a long time did not know what feelings were since he was busy acting them out as soon as there was any stirring of anxiety or depression within him. At the same time, he was giving all kinds of signals to his family, trying to gain their attention through his negative behavior in a cry for help; but they blocked out all the signs of his drug use, including the fact that his friends were actually copping in the home. He wished life to be free of any stress.

I.R. was aware of an interesting pattern of interaction between himself and his father while he was still on drugs. Some strange empathy or "ESP" seemed to exist between them since, invariably, whenever he was reaching the stage of utter exhaustion and inability to cope, his father would somehow sense this, locate him wherever he was, and bring him home. He was sent to a state mental institution the first few times, later to the Riverside, Manhattan General, and Metropolitan Hospitals. With the help of these experiences, he found he was "aging."

He described the various transitions in self-image and behavior he passed through: first was the "little gangster" stage, always in trouble and fighting, careful to be one of the boys. He was most provocative during this phase, and enjoyed starting race riots in hospitals such as Riverside because he "resented the social structure and establishment and could easily instigate power struggles between the blacks, Puerto Ricans and whites." After awhile, he became known as a troublemaker in all the hospitals, which closed their doors and refused to admit him. He learned to wield a knife skillfully and actually fought with knives at different times to prove himself. He was an "angry young man."

The second stage was that of the "hippy" addict who attempted to repress the gangster moods and avoid fighting while mainly striving for a "cool," bohemian image. Fighting was "too obvious," and he didn't go for the jail bit either, which would have appealed to him in the gangster phase. He entered into the jazz world, learned to play an instrument and was enchanted by the "cool world." The motto here was, "Tough is outmoded, be cool." He got involved with Greenwich Village hippies, began to read extensively and even did some sculpting. He strove continually to perfect his "cool" image and even reflected it in his dress; he wore a patch over one eye, a beret, and dressed in green to develop a "Jack Kerouac image." He yearned for a scar because this fitted in with his romantic image of himself. He wanted to appear knowledgeable and bohemian; he dabbled in many of the arts and associated with the "artsy-craftsy people."

The last stage occurred after five or six years when he became a hard-core addict, whole-hog. This was a really "insane" period in which he was a "full-fledged masochist with death wishes" and contemplated suicide. He viewed hospitals as a kind of sanctuary from which he could escape outside reality "in a simpler social system." There was torment and suffering in the outside world, but things were simplified in the hospital. He began to yearn to escape the desperate ritual of using drugs continuously.

I.R. was not sure why the three phases unfolded in precisely this way, but knows that the last phase is something he can hardly recollect. The impression he conveyed was of a kind of psychosis in which he was out of contact with the world and unable to remember any of the details of his daily living. Since he was high all the time, he seemed to be in a dream fantasy most of the time. It is only now when he returns to certain neighborhoods that he may suddenly smell or taste something which brings back memories he blocked out entirely, as of hiding out on roofs, being chased by police, or other distressing occurrences. He walked around as if not awake, in a zombie world, and sees it now as a terrible nightmare.

He became increasingly involved in underworld activities, sold drugs, "hustled," catted it on the streets, pimped, rarely slept, and wandered around until he was completely exhausted or "busted" and sent to jail. At such times, his father invariably reappeared to save him. The father would bathe him, "scrape me off the ground," while his mother dissociated herself and disowned him. His behavior had a most unusual effect on the father; while I.R. was busy acting out, his father began to curb his own illicit activities, came home regularly nights, became "the father of fathers," and clung to the home as if it were his nest. I.R. believes the father changed "out of a sense of guilt." There would be battles when he came home since his mother literally saw him as a "source of infection" and felt he would infest the entire home with syphilis or other vile diseases. I.R. admits he looked like a walking death at such times, with scabs and abscesses all over his body, filthy, a zombie, and so disoriented he couldn't talk coherently.

Transition to Abstinence—Transitional Phase

New York became impossible for him because he soon exhausted all his resources there. The police were looking for him because of his "dealing weight"; and a number of connections, not to mention a cluster of gangsters and "shylocks" whom he had "burned," were also out to cut his throat. He was increasingly involved in serious fights in which he either knifed or was knifed by others. He especially remembers a few "concluding scenes" which helped firm up his determination to escape from New York. He found himself increasingly restricted to a limited area of the city since he needed to avoid such places as Harlem and Greenwich Village where people were searching for him. He could no longer get into hospitals even when he threatened suicide at their door. For awhile, he stuck to the Lower East Side to hustle fags for money, then met a black kid and they decided to crack a man's house. This was one of three incidents that helped spark his desire to get away from New York.

In the first, while engaged in robbing an apartment, the police came by and he lost his shoes in his rush to escape. In another apartment house, while "taking off" with a kid, a cop followed him to the bathroom and he almost O.D.'d (he had experienced other O.D.'s in the past and related this to his desire to die). When they refused to open the door and flushed the stuff down the toilet, the cop stuck a gun in and shot the other boy in the mouth. I.R. recalls seeing all the blood and feeling certain the boy was dead, although he learned later he had not been killed. I.R. was manhandled by the policeman, who then panicked and I.R. was able to get away. The culminating scene occurred when he felt sick and decided, in desperation, to return to Harlem to score. He had already scored when he was "jumped," mugged, and stomped in a hallway by ten young kids, had his fingers smashed and teeth knocked out. It was at this juncture that he decided he must get away and headed for Synanon in the back of a pickup truck.

Adaptational Stage—The Building of Tolerance for
Abstinence Through Treatment

After he later made it at Synanon, he felt "totally omnipotent."

His craving disappeared after eighteen months there. He never-theless felt he could never leave Synanon and would never be weaned because he would be guided forever by their ideas and principles. He learned some basic "truisms" in Synanon, such as the need to tell the truth and to be honest. He also realized the need to find your own little niche in life and build on it without worrying whether the grass was greener elsewhere. He learned that he must deal with his feelings of anxiety and dis-comfort rather than act them out, and not let the ambiguity of life "punch you out of shape." You must make it as a man and be on your own two feet. He thought Synanon was largely a matter of unlearning everything he had learned in his own family and absorbing a new kind of conditioning and new way to live. For example, he had to learn that "good boys get good things" and "to lie is bad." The first year was spent amassing a tremendous amount of data "which he was then able to carry out and practice in the following two years." He is proud now that he has been off five and a half years and does not believe he can ever go back to drugs. The mere thought of having any chemical inside his body is horrifying to him. He entered Synanon with no real idea of being rehabilitated, but only to get a "free lunch," vacation, and a temporary stay, buying time until he could return safely to New York after things cooled off. He was interviewed by a number of Synanon people first ("they turned me around"). That was the end of the beginning. He resisted Synanon for about six months ("I was a real problem child"). He refused to take the jobs offered him to prove his ability to assume responsibility and was surprised that the Synanon execu-tives tolerated this. He thought now that some of the people took him on as a pet or else felt he had "potential." For the first few months, he could not adjust and "bounced off the walls." Then he did a role reversal. He did not understand all the reasons for this, but somehow he began to accept their values, change his attitude, take on jobs and do well. He recalled a turning point while he was taking a hot shower and had a vision. He suddenly thought to himself that he need never use drugs again and saw it as possible for the first time. This was a "personality flip." He also felt that a relationship formed with a girl about this time contributed to changing his attitude.

He thought he must have become "conditioned" to a new way because he was plugged into Synanon as into a new family and a new identity. He greatly enjoyed the Synanon "games," the intellectuality, and the possibility of actualizing himself. He became extremely self-righteous and messianic, having seen the light like an ex-alcoholic. This period lasted two and one-half years, well into the time he "split."

We needed to terminate the first interview at this point, and when we next met, I.R. talked briefly about his experience with girls. He had always had unsuccessful relationships with girls, thought it strange that he should have become involved with his brother's best friend's wife. At times he was dependent, like many addicts, on women for money, and even did some pimping. He found he could talk to women, charm them, and use them. He described the weird ways in which he approached women on subways, oblivious of the public. For example, he would sell girls on his "twig-magic"; that is, he used a twig as a wand, and as a kind of a charming game in order to introduce himself. He would walk over to girls, touch them with the twig and kiss them on their knees in subways. Most would be horrified and chase him away, but this became his way of "screening," since he knew he could get somewhere with those who tolerated him. His deepest relationship was with a girl who was a "thespian and lesbian—actually bisexual." I.R. claimed he did not know this for a long time; when he observed her involvement with two other girls, he hit her and left. He was still using drugs when he knew her and she herself smoked pot. He enjoyed her as a "tremendous sexual experience," was impressed to know such a beautiful girl, but was finally disillusioned and walked out on her (this is reminiscent of his traumatic relationship at twelve). He remembered this relationship because it uncovered feelings of tenderness he didn't suspect he had. He was continually stoned during this period since he used Doridens and amphetamines to boost his heroin.

As he mentioned at the first interview, things had jelled to the point where he could no longer tolerate living in New York, and this was reinforced when he took several O.D.'s and saw some of his friends die in hallways. He was quite resistant the first six months at Synanon, but then changes began taking place unconsciously and attitudinally, and the environment began establishing its power over him, emphasizing the fact that shooting dope was bad. He had to remain because he had no place to go, having even exhausted the ultimate resource of his own father who no longer wanted him home. "I'd run all the good things into a hole." He was at first preoccupied with splitting and was really buying time; he saw it as a kind of vacation until he felt better. He nevertheless found himself responding to the Synanon games, which he now believes were the single most important experience at Synanon. He found the games "emotionally challenging"; they helped consume the time and were exciting "like an emotional gang fight." These encounters ultimately moved him from a resistive attitude to a missionary and evangelic belief that Synanon was the answer to the world's ills and Chuck Diedrich, the "Second Coming." Chuck became the model father, the epitome of being a man, and I.R. struggled to identify with him. Chuck appeared as a demigod and Synanon became his religion. "I ate, drank, shit, smelled, emulated Synanon as a way of life. I found myself gaining secondary status and moving up in the organization as well." (Synanon offered rewards and punishments, including upward social mobility and the chance to become an executive and get the "champagne treatment.")

I.R. discussed his "dissipation" experiences at Synanon, by which he meant the marathon experience with the leader Jack Hirst, which he felt as a mystical experience. His description sounded positively hallucinatory and psychedelic, since he seems to have been beside himself and seemingly in a psychotic state. In the thirty-two hours spent in these marathon sessions, he lost contact with reality after seventeen hours and wasn't sure where he was, but was *aware* of a strange paradox, i.e. either he was in better control of the here and now or else he had completely lost contact with it. He recalls Chuck's coming in in a red flannel jacket and having the illusion that Chuck was a genius (which he still believes), and that he too was a genius or "wizard." He felt that he and Chuck were the only two who could understand each other, and they were having strange insights and moments of clarity which nobody else could comprehend. I.R. was strangely able to articulate many of the psychoanalytic and existential ideas of Sartre at this time though he had never read him. In discussing the "dissipations," he seemed aware of bizarre feelings he was expressing and tried to soft-pedal them, since they "sounded so insane." Some of the themes he recalled were that "man is condemned to be free, but this is his real dilemma," and he also used words like "essence," "being," and "becoming" which had previously been unknown to him.

Tolerance for Abstinence

Although by now I.R. was moving up in the Synanon system and could have had the "champagne flight" back to New York as an executive, he preferred to split in what may be characterized as his "adolescent rebellion" against Chuck Diedrich. He had been operating at Synanon on a fairly high level, but was apparently looking for cues with which to take issue, rebel, and assert his independence. He thought that "on one level, Synanon makes you a man, but on another it castrates you; it doesn't let you grow up and go out on your own." He was fighting for his masculinity since "they render you powerless." He achieved his break and fumbled his way back to New York. At that time, he thought this was the worst mistake of his life and felt utterly lost. He didn't know a soul in New York and couldn't communicate with anybody, thought everybody insane, and saw New York as a festering abscess of emotional disease." He was depressed and felt as a complete stranger. He returned to the "scenes of his crime," not to test if he were cured, but to see what it was like through his new set of glasses. What he saw revolted him. He drifted about New York wondering how anyone could grow up healthy in an environment like this. He even went home. The family was terrified when they first saw him since they knew he had left Synanon on his own and thought "the monster has returned." They couldn't accept the possibility that he might really be off drugs and didn't care to have him back. He talked with them and didn't react to their "insanity" as before, but was able to control himself. His parents continually searched his eyes and were leery that he might be back on drugs. He had the strange idea his parents were disappointed that he was doing well and making it.

Each week saw progress since I.R. was working and saving money. He even bought a car. He first worked with adolescent boys but found this boring; then he felt he would like to express the ideas of Synanon "with modifications," by working with "squares" as well as addicts in the community. He disliked Dr. Ramirez' program in New York City since he felt the system was too much like Synanon's, "but with more bullshit since they didn't have the right to take on these concepts themselves because they hadn't earned it." He also refused to go to Daytop Village, and helped found his own group with other ex-addicts. He was trying to avoid the dogma of Synanon and their total preoccupation with their own image as the "New Order." I.R. appeared to have a strong preference for working with professionals and pursuing middle-class goals since he finally became involved in working in professional programs. He still feels attached to Chuck Diedrich and Synanon and has not resolved his ambivalent feelings, but he believes he may never do so. He is still awed by his dissipation experiences, which were the greatest thing that ever happened to him, verging on the mystical and hallucinatory. There are still elements of grandiosity in I.R. as in the belief he is a "wizard" or guru. He is on better terms with his family and is accepted by them. He is also closer to his brother from whom he was alienated before. He is steadily moving ahead as an executive, is utterly down on all drugs, and is comfortable in the square culture, with some modifications.

CASE OF I.R.   SYNANON

Brotman-Freedman
   1. Normal conventionality   —
   2. Criminality history   —
   3. Family conventionality   —
   4. Friends conventionality   +
   Characterization: "Hustler"

Chein Typology

Drug use served to block out feelings of depression and anxiety and awareness of problems related to his parents. I.R. saw his mother as destructive and the father as seductive; related in a feminine-passive fashion to the father. He was scapegoated in the family and was viewed as "the monster."

Life Cycle

Close to confirmed street addict.

Social Milieu

New York to Nevada to California to New York.

Cloward-Ohlin

No real question of blocked opportunity. Certainly "retreatist" in refusing conventional goals.

Case of Mrs. B.

This rather appealing Puerto Rican woman in her thirties, who is employed as a staff member of a residential center, seemed exceedingly closed in and detached from the rather terrible details she was describing in her past life and admitted it was hard for her to visualize them now. She preferred not to think back and was therefore quite resistant so that it proved difficult to get at the underlying feelings and motivations. The surface impression was of a very composed girl who had inadvertently or even innocently been pulled into dangerous and destructive behavior. As we spoke, she showed some awareness of having had a high tolerance for deviancy: she had been struggling with many problems; she had identified with an acting-out mother and felt rejected by her father.

Familial and Social Background

Her first use started in 1933, shortly after she married a man who was a user and seller. She claimed she was unaware of this when she married him at the age of eighteen. At one point, she projected blame onto her husband; but later felt that, even if she hadn't married him, she would have sought out drugs. She was aware of some "wildness" in herself as in her mother. As a teenager, she loved fast crowds and dancing, but was also torn between different images, one of wanting to go to school to be something in the nature of a professional or semi-professional; the other, running around with a wild gang.

Her parents were divorced, as she says, "since I was born." She attributed this to adultery on her mother's part. Strangely, she said she had never questioned her mother about it since the mother was now devoutly religious and the father was too. So many years had elapsed, also, that when she finally "made it," she was reluctant to reopen the question. She admitted this could be a rationalization. She was born a week before her mother was fourteen. The father was much older, but they were legally married and were distant cousins from the same area of Puerto Rico. She added that she was born during the depression, as if to emphasize the bad circumstances surrounding her birth.

Her mother had been wild; she was always sneaking off and playing hooky and running around with a fast group and her grandmother thought it best to get her married even though she was barely thirteen years old. When they came to New York, they met the father who had a steady job. He held this job for many years so he must have been a stable person. He always took responsibility for his daughter, contributing to her support. She was conceived before the parents' marriage, but this did not stop the mother. She recalled the facts surrounding their separation when she was only four years old. The father was suspicious of the mother and followed her to a party, bringing in the police after him. There was a wild scene and possibly some violence, although she cannot recall the details. For a few months, she lived with her maternal grandmother and aunt, but then was brought by the father to live with her godmother. She did not see her mother for a long time after this, although she was aware the mother must have been living somewhere in the neighborhood. This is all quite hazy now. The father came to see her every night. She admitted she was not anxious to find out more about the mother for fear of finding out "too much." She now hoped for the same courtesy from her children; the important thing was what she did with her own life now. She admitted she had often wondered about the person with whom her mother first committed adultery.

The father remarried when she was seven and she thereafter

led a bitter life with the stepmother, a very strange and disturbed woman, rejecting, critical, and abusive, who beat her quite often with her hands or a broom. She recalled her mother once told her that the father never looked at her until she was two because she was not a boy. He never had any other children and always wanted a boy to carry on the family name. She thus saw herself as a failure from the beginning and felt she must be a burden to her mother, who was too young to care for her and never had a childhood of her own. She lived with her father for seven years after he remarried and never knew where her mother was. Occasionally, a mysterious woman appeared out of the blue, usually when she was returning from school, hugged and kissed her and gave her money and things. She remembers being happy yet upset about it, and finally became aware that this must be her natural mother. She recalled one incident when the father took her to a dance and her mother happened to be there. The mother created an uproar because she saw the stepmother hitting her. The mother remained a vague figure; and she constantly heard hostile remarks from the father and stepmother who tried to prejudice her against the mother.

In describing her life with the stepmother, she said she was beaten "every day" and the woman treated her like Cinderella. On the other hand, the father developed a "sort of closeness to her," treating her like daddy's little girl and playmate. In fact, the father "idolized" her and told her she was the smartest, prettiest girl in the world. The stepmother was jealous of this and hit her to vent her jealousy and anger. The stepmother was very peculiar and did not allow her to have playmates or even to speak to other children. She hated living in this house since the stepmother was too orderly and "cluttery" about everything. She collected things and never threw them out, had to have everything covered up with sheets, and kept the shades drawn, and she didn't understand why. She also put locks on everything. To this day, Mrs. B. cannot stand to have anything locked. Mrs. B's description of her family life appears as a stereotype of the oedipal situation since the father doted on her, took her with him everywhere, and bought her clothing. The stepmother was a typical witch or ogre who made her wear the terrible clothing she sewed on the machine and use the good clothing only for going out. The stepmother also made her cook, iron, and clean (although she admitted she was not really overworked). What was more serious was that she was not allowed to go out and play with others. The breakdown of the stepmother occurred, interestingly, on the very day when Mrs. B. was being married, so that the father could not attend her wedding, but visited the stepmother instead in the hospital.

Looking back, she thought that, as a girl, from the age of twelve to fourteen, she had been quite ordinary, simply wanting friends and boyfriends. She was attending junior high school and it took her ten minutes to get home, but the stepmother made a tremendous point of her coming home immediately. Things were crystallized one day when she defiantly said, "To hell with it," and came home late. She found the door locked and overheard her father and stepmother saying they would not let her in until she learned her lesson. She left the home "never to come back." In fact, she went to a girlfriend's house and one of the boys in the crowd, whom she liked, said that she could not walk the streets. He offered to help her find her mother, and so she began going to different houses until, late at night, she finally located the grandmother and the mother. The next period was rather happy since she stayed with the grandmother and mother who were then boarding with a family. They subsequently moved with some other aunts into a shared apartment. Mrs. B. said she had begun to suffer and lose weight because the grandmother had begun working and she was left alone in the house. Her mother took her to the police station to report that she was missing, and the police allowed the mother to take her home. The father subsequently came looking for her at the grandmother's and was quite incensed. He told her she could either return with him or stay with the women. Mrs. B. said she preferred to stay with the mother, and the father yielded.

She was quite content in this setup and even liked the man her mother had married. The mother and aunt worked and the grandmother took care of her and, in fact, acted like her real mother; she gave her "unconditional love," and was generally a happy and joyous woman, never angry. However, Mrs. B. had many battles with the mother, a cold and strict person who was trying to impose on the daughter the sanctions she could not observe herself. What came out was Mrs. B.'s feeling that her mother had never loved her. She therefore continually tested the mother, making excessive demands and claiming the mother rejected her. She was upset when the mother later returned to Puerto Rico with the stepfather. Mrs. B. stayed with the grandmother, preferring to remain with her. She continued this way until seventeen, attending school, taking academic subjects since she had aspirations to be a nurse. She went to the movies and to football games and lived a "typical teenage life" until she was graduated from high school. At this point, a crisis ensued with the father, who again came into the picture when she graduated. She wished to go to nursing school and needed money for it. Her father was supposed to bring her the money for her graduation expenses and tuition. When he failed to show, she went to the beach with friends. Her father waited until she returned, but was furious because he felt she cared more about her friends than him, and said he was not going to give her the money. She felt terribly rejected, said she wouldn't go to nursing school and wouldn't need the money. She could do things on her own. She registered at a local college, but could not continue because she had no money for books or tuition. She had been working nights as a busgirl to support the schooling. She discovered that she didn't know how to do anything as far as work was concerned since she had never studied commercial subjects. She found work and continued until her marriage.

Addiction—Initial Experimentation

She had been working and dancing a great deal, moving with a fast crowd and going to dancehalls where she first met her husband. She was very excited about his car, a Cadillac, and his appearance. He was Puerto Rican and good looking, but much older (the exact age difference between her father and mother). He was flashy, and she was dazzled; she succumbed completely when he took her night-clubbing. It was a whirlwind romance, and she married him within ten days. About a month after the marriage, the apartment was raided, and she learned then that her husband and the two other people staying with them were drug users and sellers. She was arrested along with them and held in the Women's House of Detention, a very humiliating experience. Although she claimed she had known nothing of what was happening, she admitted that she had been questioned by her aunt, who wondered what the husband did, where he got his elaborate furniture and car from since he did not seem to be working. She admitted he also had "crooked-looking friends." Now she realized there was much to be suspicious of, but she had simply blocked it out. It emerged that her husband was a big-time dealer known to the police, and the whole story became front page news with her picture next to her husband's. The prison didn't believe that she wasn't an addict and put her in with other addicts. Her family came and bailed her out, and she felt terrible, though not enough to prevent her from returning to the husband when he was released on bail. He said he didn't want her involved in his illegal life. She therefore went back to him while the charges were still pending, but there were large legal bills to be paid. Her husband asked her whether she couldn't start prostituting, and she agreed because she was scared. She was frightened of her husband because he had hit her several times and threatened her when she showed she was discontented and wished to return to the grandmother.

She began using drugs now "for many reasons": she was unhappy, hated her friends, and hated prostituting.

She had been married in a double wedding; the other man was also a drug addict and seller and his wife a prostitute. She was now taken to the home of this woman, who instructed her in the techniques of prostituting. Her husband didn't know she had begun using drugs, since he never saw her, but one of his friends showed her how to snort. They first pushed her into it saying she was really a little girl and didn't know anything, and why didn't she try heroin. The husband's friend put some stuff on his nail, and she snorted it. Her action was not to be sick, but rather to become extroverted and happy. She explained she had been very introverted and unable to move toward people. The drugs had a remarkable adaptive value in that she could deal better with people and it also blocked out her guilt about prostituting. When she again tried to visit this friend to get more stuff, she was advised not to come since she would get them into trouble. There was dope in her own house and she needn't come to them. He told her where her husband kept the stuff and she stole some every day, snorting it, not using the needle until she was addicted without realizing it.

At first she thought she had a cold. Then when she got a call to work for the madam of a house, she said she couldn't come because of her cold. The madam told her that she didn't have a cold, but was actually addicted, and suggested that she come over and she would give her drugs to make her feel better. Mrs. B. felt terrible because she realized she was "hooked." Her husband still didn't know she was on the stuff. Things continued this way until the husband was rearrested. In fact, both were arrested when the "Feds" came in because of a sale. She later learned that one of his best friends had "stooled" on the husband and her. The "Government" seemed to know everything about them at Foley Square, but she was let go. She recalls a very fatherly Federal Narcotics Bureau captain who treated her as if she were his own daughter and gave her paternal advice; he hadn't had children, but if this had happened to a daughter of his, he would want her to get a chance at rehabilitation. The husband had registered a car in her name. The captain gave her the money her husband had in his possession and advised her to sell the car and use the money herself. She blew the money very quickly on drugs. Her husband was sentenced to a year's hospitalization. She herself later went to Lexington, Kentucky, as part of her rehabilitation. When her husband found that she was an addict, he seemed to be not at all concerned and was worried only about his car.

Addiction

She found she was now becoming more and more immersed in drugs, taking all she could get—sometimes three to four quarter-ounce bags a day. In fact, she ruined the linings of her nostrils and, to this day, cannot taste or smell anything. She stayed at Lexington three months since it was the only hospital available at the time, and then left with a "fast crowd" going to Boston. This was an impulsive action with no real plan except to stay with drugs and possibly sell them. She was stranded when her friends abandoned her, and then she went to Philadelphia with a man because she was needed there as an emissary to transport drugs. In Philadelphia, her male contact was arrested, and she was again alone. She was arrested for "internal possession" and jailed.

She returned home. Her mother was in Puerto Rico and knew she was a drug addict. She believed her father didn't know as yet. She stayed with her grandmother who was willing to take her back, and things were alright for awhile. She began working, but soon began using drugs again, was again arrested and jailed for felonious possession. She received a three-year sentence, fifteen months of which were spent in the Women's House of Detention. When she was paroled, she again began using, working, prostituting, and shoplifting. Her mother came back to New York at this time, began living with another man in a common-law relationship and was soon pregnant by him. Mrs. B. attempted to live with them for a short time, but didn't get along with the man and moved out. It was at this point that Mrs. B. admitted that her natural father drank and engaged in weekend binges, but she added that he was never abusive and never drank at home. He was never a "real" alcoholic and he worked regularly.

She began living with a man herself, a former friend of her husband's who was also an addict and a pusher. She became pregnant and resumed shoplifting; she was rearrested and sent to jail as a violator to complete her sentence. She came home in 1959 and began working for a union and joined their association. Even while here, she was still using drugs; she now could always work and use drugs. She had begun a "needle habit" in Boston because money was short, and they showed her how to do it. Upon release from jail, she discovered she was pregnant. Her boyfriend had stopped using but was selling. She was leading a dual life. Their apartment was raided, and they were again arrested. She had her baby while out on bail, awaiting trial. She was again sentenced to prison. She stopped to wonder that all this could have happened to her since it seemed as if it were a dream now. She was institutionalized for two years and then released. She violated parole and was resentenced for using drugs. She found it hard now to keep track of her endless arrests, imprisonments, hospitalizations, and the things she needed to do related to using, prostituting, and shoplifting.

In 1966, she was arrested for felonious assault. This had to do with a policeman who was a "sick person," who had abused other prisoners, especially addicts. When he found her prostituting, he beat her brutally on the head and hands so that she was terribly battered. She brought charges against him, but when he brought other policemen to testify that she was an addict and a prostitute, she retreated and did not press the charges. She felt she had now reached "rock bottom." Between the courts and the judges and the jails and the hospitals, she could no longer keep track of things and felt completely out of control. Things came to a head when the judge attempted to impose a very severe sentence because of her history and because her attempts at rehabilitation had not worked. However, under pressure from some good people, especially a priest, the judge relented and decreed three years' probation instead. To cap things, she discovered she was pregnant once again. She tried work without using drugs, but soon found herself drinking and taking pills, barbiturates, etc. She really hit bottom, no longer cared what happened, and gave up hope. She developed toxemia; her teeth were rotten; she was full of abscesses; and she did not know what was happening with her pregnancy. She called the priest who took her to Bellevue. She could hardly walk because of her toxemia. She found a woman psychiatrist there involved with addiction who persuaded her to try an addict-directed residential center. She did and related well because it helped her deal with her problems and understand more about her relationship with her parents. Still, she saw this as a "rehashing" and going back to the past, which she was reluctant to do. She liked the encounters with the ex-addicts and was able to understand more about her relationship with her parents. She was able to see through the traps they set for themselves in order to destroy themselves, and to talk more freely about her feelings for the first time. Interestingly, she stressed the educational aspects of the center and the reentry phase in which she was now involved. She described this in terms of being reeducated and trained "in a professional sense." She identified increasingly as a woman and felt she had a special obligation to work with other women and help them straighten out their lives. She was concerned that so few Puerto Rican women became involved and hoped that this could be improved. She was learning to handle herself better; her craving had lessened, and when tensions came, she knew how to deal with them. In the past, she had blocked out her feelings with drugs since they were so painful. She felt terribly guilty about her prostitution and about the children; she thought drugs had been an escape from reality and responsibility and that they were self-destructive and a slow death.

She was in conflict about the twin images she had, one of a junkie, the other of a stable person who feared responsibility yet always managed to work in a clerical or professional capacity. Throughout her drug addiction, she somehow maintained the image of herself as a white collar worker and was anxious to achieve it in spite of "the life."

In reviewing what helped her "make it," she felt that she had hit "rock bottom." She realized that she had no choice: she must either die or do something with her life, and these were the absolute alternatives. The "moment of truth" came when the judge described her as a "hopeless case" and tried to put her away. This became a challenge to her, and she wanted above all to prove him wrong. Having children had been her way of proving to her mother that she was indeed a woman. Still, she hadn't taken good care of them. In many ways she seemed to be following in the footsteps of her mother. She added that she looked exactly like her mother and had a bad temper like her.

She loves the encounters now though she gets "beat up" in them. She has been assuming a parental role, playing mama or papa to the kids, but is tiring of this role and would like to move on, possibly leaving the whole addiction system. She wants to go back to school and fulfill herself away from the addiction scene. In every person, in spite of death wishes, there must be a spark to "make it." She was finally, overwhelmingly unhappy about her addiction and wanted to do something with herself and possibly help others.

CASE OF MRS. B.   THEREPEUTIC COMMUNITY

Brotman-Freedman Typology

   1. Normal conventionality   —
   2. Criminality and hustling   —
   3. Family conventionality   —
   4. Friends conventionality   —
   Characterization: "Hustler"

Chein's Typology

Problems with mother and father. She felt rejected and rebelled. Classified adults everywhere as "good" or "bad" parents.

Life Cycle

Reached "rock bottom" as a street addict and prostitute though held on to some square values.

Social Milieu

Puerto Rico to New York.

Cloward-Ohlin

Had access to upward mobility. Relinquished it, by dropping out of school.

NARCOTICS ANTAGONIST—CYCLAZOCINE

Case of Mr. R.

Mr. R. is a thirty-seven-year-old, Italian middle-class musician from Brooklyn, boyish-looking and appealing. He is a graduate of a chemotherapy program in Brooklyn and is being groomed for a position as a research assistant or assistant group leader in the program. It should be mentioned that a good deal is known about him through his participation in group therapy sessions.

Mr. R. thinks he is "unique" in that he has always been in control of his habit and had a constant motivation to stop. For many years, he was involved in different forms of treatment to help him with his problems, but felt he finally found it in this program. He describes "three elements" in what helped him get off drugs:

1. *Chemical*—though he had motivation to stop previously, the yen and craving still remained. The chemical eliminated or inhibited his craving and acting out, and he had this extra support to bolster his motivation.

2. *Private treatment*—which he received in the past and which he continued here, gave him a chance to understand and work out his deeper problems.

3. *Group therapy*—made it possible for him to implement the insights he had gained through individual therapy. He thought the group therapy was, at this point, the most important element since it provided a unique experience he had not had before.

Addiction Set—Predisposing Social and Psychological Factors

In discussing his history, the word "family" became the leitmotif which played a key role in his life. The group experience became important as a replication of his original family experience: he viewed me as the father figure, a "man who adhered strongly to principles, which was mixed with a great deal of compassion." (The image of his own father was very confused; he saw him as a rather arbitrary, irrational, and at times, violent person to whom he could relate only by being passive and feminine. At the same time, the father sought him out as a favorite and was often quite seductive with him.) He saw the co-therapist, male, as a mother figure, understanding, sympathetic, yet as a very pliable and flexible person who could be "wedged." (He saw his own mother this way, though she is much more "ridiculous" and seductive with him.) He could not express his hostility to the co-therapist and felt he had never worked out his underlying hostility to his mother. He saw the ex-addict assistant group leader as his older brother, whom he admired as "stable" and forceful, a model he could envy. He viewed other members of the group as being like his middle brother, very unstable and acting out their neurotic behavior. He saw a female member as his sister, completely detached, and enclosed in herself without real contact or understanding, as if wrapped in a "tight shell." He has no strong identification with her; she is just a "female." The whole group experience gave him a chance to carry out the things learned in private treatment and to overcome the things which separated him from life.

In discussing the factors which pushed him into drugs, he reiterated that "everything is family with me." The great impelling motive in his life has been to be part of a family, accepted and loved. By becoming a drug user, he was joining a big family which he then admired. He recalled there had never been a place for him in his own family; he didn't even have a bed of his own so that he usually found himself sleeping either with his brother or mother, or wherever else he could find a place. Unfortunately, the brother and mother used him seductively, the brother having homosexual relations with him, and the mother being openly seductive with him as well. The drug culture then became his "big mama" and his connection. When I wondered why he had to choose a *negative* family, he explained that he was unwilling to compete in "the family of the world"; drugs offered him a place where he would not need to compete and could be accepted and revered on his own terms. In his own family, in spite of all the hang-ups, he had been the good little boy. And he now continued this image by becoming "the saint in the drug world." "I dignified their actions by being ethical." He never "burned" anybody, never acted dishonorably, and everybody could rely on him. Mr. R. has a very great need to be loved. He picked up on his fear of failure and of competing in the square world. The drug culture also served as an introduction to the world of work since he was able to meet with good musicians before he had actually proven himself and without the need to compete with them. He would have been afraid to compete with them on a musical level if the drugs had not served as a cover. He realizes now that he began using drugs at a time when life was completely empty for him before his marriage. His father was dead; his mother was working; his brother was out of town; his sister was married; and he was alone and needed something to substitute for this loss of family.

Tolerance for Potential Addiction

EXPERIMENTATION STAGE—IRREGULAR USE. He became an addict because it "suited the direction I wanted to go in." He did not want to continue in high school because this was a competitive situation. He had friends who were using alcohol, but he didn't continue associating with them and wanted to drop out of school. He finished high school only with difficulty and was greatly relieved. His big dream all through high school was to live without stress. Drugs helped to erase any pressures since they anesthetized him, and he had the secondary gains of belonging and acceptance in a new culture. The social life, "family," and acceptance were thus the major elements in his becoming a drug addict. He constantly used drugs "in a social sense," with others present. It was not until he was far into the drug culture that he became a "loner" and "private junkie," copping and getting drugs all by himself.

He began at about the age of eighteen or nineteen, first while he was with a band. The vocalist was a black musician, a big-time man, more talented and successful and better recognized at the time than he. Mr. R. was very pleased that this man should accept him as a friend, and this man implemented it by helping him snort drugs. Mr. R. continued to snort and didn't start shooting until a year later. He thought this was related to his desire to be accepted into a new hip group of musicians who were further ahead and recognized. He had witnessed other men using the needle many times, but never thought of doing it himself until a friend "skin-popped" him once. When he returned from a trip to the city, he contacted a couple who were both addicts and were using "dirty spikes," which were clogged and dangerous. He had previously watched another friend, who later died of an O.D., clean the needles with vinegar; and he, like a good housewife, became preoccupied with cleaning their needles for them and participating in the ritual of preparation. He only snorted first for a couple of years and was content with this.

ADAPTATION STAGE. Additional motives for using drugs came in as he made a miserable marriage, though doing very well professionally. His wife was a drag, and he needed a buffer, which drugs served admirably to provide. He in time also became fearful of the withdrawal, and this, too, helped keep him on drugs. Whenever he got hooked, he became terribly cold and needed to put on heavy clothes and stand near the stove, feeling isolated and frozen until he got his shot again. To avoid criticism from his wife, he involved her in his drug use so that she was soon chipping too. He was never really worried about her since he knew he was her connection, and he could control how much drugs she got. In fact, she never did become fully involved and dropped use after some initial experimentation. In discussing his craving, Mr. R. thought it was largely a matter of rationalization, since if something good happened he wanted to celebrate, and if it was something bad, he needed to compensate; there was always need for drugs.

He had used marijuana, which he liked because it made him creative and was related to his music; it stimulated him intellectually. He put down cocaine, saying it made him "nervous." He enjoyed alcohol because it was a "social thing," and he was never a lone drinker. He preferred Dexamyl® in combination with alcohol as part of a social scene, though not by itself. He tried sleeping pills once, and it slowed him down, but he didn't like the feeling of being sluggish and apathetic. He thought, on the whole, that he had been trying to free himself to function better, and heroin did this for him. He always had a terrible complex about success and managed to sabotage his own efforts since he was afraid of acting independently, being responsible, and functioning as an individual instead of hiding behind the drug culture and drugs.

REGULAR USE-ADDICTED. He began using a needle and continued for three or four years. He found himself getting sucked into the addiction culture through a school friend. For the first time now, through the connection, he had real access to drugs and became seriously dependent on it.

Transition to Abstinence-Recidivism

The first sign of trauma occurred when his connection O.D.'d at the age of twenty-six. This started him thinking that it could happen to him, too, and that he needed to stop using drugs before he died. Before then, he had had infantile feelings of omnipotence and believed he was immortal and that nothing could touch him, but this trauma shook him up. He had never been "busted," never hospitalized for detox, except for one occasion when he himself O.D.'d. There were many feelings impelling him to continue using since the acceptance of the addict group was vital to his existence, and through his "family" he could perpetuate the family structure he so desperately needed. Heroin also gave him a physical feeling of euphoria that all was right with the world and that he need not worry about pressure. He did not stop to wonder whether he was oppressed because drugs always kept him high.

From this beginning, the history is rather consistent since he never lost sight of his goal of wanting to be straight, and he pursued it through different therapies. He began with Freudian treatment, but disliked it since the therapist was impersonal and unloving, and he could not relate to him. He believes this kind of "detached" Freudian therapy is not good for addicts.

He sought other treatment. He emphasized that he has always sought a framework and firm structure in life, and when he found this was lacking in his treatment, he could not fully relate himself to it. He believes drug addiction is a very specialized sickness for which you need controls, and treatment which lacks these controls and deals with more general problems cannot be effective for addiction. He felt that chemotherapy was the answer for him and that he had made it now and would continue to grow out of his addiction. He especially liked the structure in the program; he also liked the feeling that he did not need to hide anything and could come out with all his problems and still be accepted.

In further interviews, Mr. R. was able to elaborate on some of the elements mentioned earlier which perpetuated his remaining in the drug culture:

1. His family problem and the relationship with his wife.

2. The fact that he was becoming relatively successful and needed to "dull the terror of success."

At the time he was doing best professionally, he was also using the most. This was when he was younger. In answering my question as to what made him come to me for therapy, he replied that the drugs had somehow begun working in reverse since he was now out of control and beginning to lose his grip. He thought this emanated from the realization that he was entirely dependent on drugs in his work; it wasn't he who was doing well in music, but rather the drugs. If he should stop using drugs, his music would deteriorate. Naturally, he could not prove his case, since if he stopped using drugs he would become sick and then play terribly, and he could never get beyond this point. He therefore came to treatment out of desperation since this was the worst time "and the best time in my life." It was the first time he had made a contract with himself to admit openly that he was an addict and in need of help.

Mr. R. indicated that he had made many unsuccessful attempts to get off in the past, and, while he had not hit "rock bottom," had lost his self-respect. He was proud that he always maintained his family ties, worked, and never did anything unethical to get his drugs. Although he had a number of experiences with therapy, it never worked because he had never admitted to himself that he was a junkie. His rationalization for seeking treatment had been that it was for general self-improvement and enlightenment, or because of family problems. It was only "incidentally" because he had a "slight drug problem." He was afraid to use the needle after he O.D.'d and resorted to sniffing, which gave him a further element of control since he could stop if his nose became irritated. He was beginning to taper off at the time he first saw me, but was still quite dependent and was using other substances such as Dolophine®, cough medicine, and whatever else he could get his hands on.

He realized, however, that he had always been a "secretive junkie" and could never admit it to others or to himself, "out of his guilt." Having the problem out in the open made it easier now to face things himself and to seek real help.

In looking back, he thought that the interaction with his wife perpetuated his drug use since the marital situation was intolerable. He realizes now that it "takes two to tango," and he played a role in creating this intolerable situation (which drugs made more tolerable) and made it impossible to abstain from use. His marriage was a "sick egotism" and a symptom of what was basically wrong with him; that is, if someone shows a need for him, he will go out of his way to do something for them, even to the extent of marrying them. The more his wife was dependent on him, the more he needed to give back to her, though resenting it all the time. The relationship with his wife is far better now since she was referred to a local clinic and has benefitted from treatment. They can now both short-circuit their neurotic interactions and can stop clobbering each other, while accepting responsibility for what they are doing. He believes his use affected the children, one of whom experimented with marijuana and other drugs. He feels he will never use drugs again since there have been many distressing experiences recently which he has tolerated without undue problems.

In a subsequent interview, Mr. R. was asked to answer specific points, such as why he had preferred heroin. He thought that it "affected him more physically," and he was able to work and function on it better than with other substances. In explaining what led to his frequent relapses, he attributed this to the continuing factors in the home situation—the relationship with the wife. He was also aware that he had enjoyed the feeling of strength which his wife's insatiable dependency gave him, while resenting it at the same time. The drug further satisfied his craving, which for him consisted in getting through with what he had to do, i.e. tolerating pressure and getting ego support for these pressures. He was aware of a number of rituals in drug use, but said he never really subscribed to them, and in this sense was not a typical addict. He hated injecting himself with a needle, for example, and, whenever possible, got other

people to do it for him. He hated the marks left by the needle
and was terrified of missing the vein. In terms of heroin's effect
on sex, he said it enhanced his virility since he could go for
extended periods of more than three-quarters of an hour and
satisfy his wife. However, he missed the orgasm himself, which
was often not possible under heroin use.

In terms of the effect of heroin on his aggression, he felt he
was more aggressive, especially when using it in music or for
social functioning. As regards pain, he said drugs played no
role since he could always withstand a good deal of pain. Regarding abstinence, he said he had never aimed for total obliteration
of himself and was always concerned about controlling the extent
of his use and not becoming a street junkie. He was, in fact,
able to do this by avoiding hospitals and jails, working to support
his habit, and maintaining ties with wife and children. In regard
to therapy, in the past he kidded himself by thinking he was going
to get off drugs entirely, whereas he was simply trying to control
the habit and maintain it at a moderate level. When asked what
made the difference in this chemotherapy program, he thought
it was the fact that so many people were, for the first time,
genuinely concerned about him. He no longer felt alone. He
had the feeling of being enveloped in a warm family that was
genuinely worried about him and anxious to pull him out of
his drug use. He saw the chemotherapy as "family therapy,"
enjoyed the whole climate, and wanted to remain a member of
this family by becoming an assistant therapist.

Regarding other methods of treatment, he was broad-minded
and said that if they could help any addicts at all, they should
be tried. As far as he was concerned, Synanon could not help
since he was afraid he would lose his identity there. He also
saw it as involved with a tremendous number of rituals and a
"coldness" in which he could not function. In regard to methadone maintenance, he said it would have been great for him
when he was not really serious about stopping. However, he
sees methadone maintenance as only a half-way measure, and he
wants to get off all drugs as soon as possible.

In discussing how he became an ex-addict, he felt that one

must have the motivation and willingness to trade a life of drug use for something better. He felt that no generalizations could be made about how to become an ex-addict since it was so individual. This is why it is so difficult to separate out what program is good for whom since each person may need different things at different times to function in the addiction system.

Discussion

The crucial factor in this Italian middle-class patient seems to relate to the idea of family and belonging, being accepted, and liked. The motif of family recurs regularly throughout his addiction and figures largely in his later efforts to help himself. Mr. R. does not see himself as a "typical drug addict," and, in fact, seems more representative of the so-called "hidden drug abusers" since he was never hospitalized or arrested in his many years of drug use. He worked regularly and supported his family; he was able to stop using the needle and rely on snorting after taking an O.D. His wife was involved with him in his early heroin use, but never really needed drugs, never became addicted, and was able to discontinue without difficulty. She still smokes pot occasionally.

Mr. R. made it with the help of chemotherapy and is being prepared to work as an assistant group therapist. This kind of recognition is very important to him. To Mr. R. the group experience has been most important recently since it reconstituted the family, and he felt there was a "real concern for" the person not the patient. In terms of early family dynamics, the mother was very seductive, and the father was at times, too, although he more often appeared as a stern, even violent and threatening figure, capable of terrible rages. Mr. R. related passively like a woman to win the father's affection and always needed to repress his hostility and win everybody's affection by being a "good guy." There was literally no place for him in the home, so that he needed to sleep in different beds, being used seductively by the family.

Drugs became the "big Mama" through the drug connection; Papa was the Law. When asked why he needed to find a negative family, he said he was unwilling to compete in the "family of the world" because of his fear of failure. He felt accepted in this drug world and became the good guy of drugs, "saint of the group," ethical, and respected. Drugs were actually adaptive and useful to him in the work world since they became the link through which he could associate himself with excellent musicians when he was still a novice himself.

In fact, Mr. R. was never really comfortable in this family of drugs, as in his original family, and never lost sight of his goal of getting off drugs. His history shows him getting involving with many different kinds of treatment before he found chemotherapy. The thing he believes really distinguished this program from others was the feeling of a strong structured program which was truly interested in him as a human being and not merely as a drug addict.

He had fears of success and the responsibilities it entails, and drugs served admirably to stifle these fears and impede success. He also felt whatever success he experienced in his music was due to the drugs and not to him; if he stopped using, his music would deteriorate. The change came when he could admit to himself that he was truly an addict, sick, and in need of help. A most important factor was his realization that he could find a new family which would accept him and help him make it.

CASE OF MR. R.   CYCLAZOCINE

Brotman-Freedman Typology
    1. Normal conventionality $+$
    2. Criminal history $+$
    3. Family conventionality $+$
    4. Friend conventionality $+$
    Classification: "Conformist"

Chein's Typology
    Mr. R. was seeking love, belonging, and a family of which he could be a part. He is essentially conformist with square goals though fearful of stress, competition, and success.

Life Cycle
    A "hidden drug abuser," middle-class, essentially square, and conformist in all areas except for drug use.

Social Milieu
New York.

Cloward-Ohlin
Never lost sight of square values though fearful of competition and success. Upward mobility was available to him.

METHADONE MAINTENANCE

Case of Mr. N.

Mr. N. is a short man of Puerto Rican background; his face is somewhat puffy and sallow. He affects dark glasses and looks tense and troubled.

Addiction Set—Predisposing Social and Psychological Factors

In discussing his history, Mr. N. promised to "start at the beginning." When he began, he knew nothing about drugs. However, his brother who was two years older, was already using. Mr. N. recalled the exact moment he discovered his brother was sniffing heroin. He wasn't sure what the brother was doing, but knew it was something "not good." He threatened to squeal to the parents, and the brother, in his "sixteen-year-old-mind," thought that the way to prevent this was by involving N. in his addiction. After some coaxing, N. was persuaded to try it too, and this was his first experience. He got sick, threw up, and "wanted to drink milk." Instead, the brother told him to swallow it when it came down his nose into his throat, and this was the wind-up. His parents were both working at the time, and N. got so twisted that, when they came in, he was reading his comic book upside down. The brother himself had only been using a short time, and after this experience his friends began coming more freely to the home.

N. looked up to his brother and these friends; they were like "idols" to him. They affected an aloof manner and dressed well, and he tried to imitate them since it was something new and "cool." Before then, he had been a regular kid, very square, and concerned with sports, but he now fell in love with the cool image and the rituals associated with it. He described these rituals as dressing conservatively, using hip words, and listening to jazz or bop, which was popular at the time. It also meant copying their mannerisms. For some reason, one mannerism particularly stood out in his mind: the boys all had neatly pressed, usually new handkerchiefs, which they either held carefully folded in their hands or else put to their faces. This seems reminiscent of the way the aristocrats of France and Britain used their handkerchiefs, or perhaps, the ladies their fans. When they sat down, they did it slowly and carefully, first folding the creases in their pants to make sure everything was exactly in place. They were always in control and affected a knowledgeable air, superior to everybody else, walking slowly, never hurrying. There was a feeling that they were supremely slick, in the know, and with vast experience in everything.

N. began hanging around the candy stores where these boys associated and developed feelings of superiority over the friends with whom he had formerly played ball, because he was "into something they weren't into." He became engulfed in the new rituals and image, and felt this was an exciting world, different from his previous life. He had been a very good student in school and had certificates of merit and attendance. He was always in the "I" class, that is, with the smartest group, and stayed home at night or else played checkers with his father. He was always home early, too. In the course of two years, however (around the period of puberty), a number of things began happening at the same time. He was no longer sure which came first although he thinks his participation in gang fights preceded his drug use, or possibly they were simultaneous. Here, too, the brother served as his model since he introduced him to his gang and actually coached him in gang fighting, teaching him to dress the part before he came to a meeting to discuss the strategy for the gang fight. He didn't stick out the gang phase, however, after he got into heroin. He is still unable to comprehend the sudden transition from good boy to bad boy, since he did a complete reversal from everying he had liked before. A big factor was his desire to belong, and this was the "in" thing to do in the neighborhood. This was the period after World

War II, and to N. it appeared to be the only way to be accepted. He also admired his brother and followed in his steps; he was delighted to be accepted by him and his friends as an equal.

Tolerance for Potential Addiction

EXPERIMENTATION STAGE—IRREGULAR USE. Mr. N. thought it unusual that he started immediately with heroin rather than first fooling around with pot or pills. About a year and a half after using heroin, he also tried pot and "guesses" he liked it. He still uses pot although he has stopped all other drug use since getting into the methadone maintenance program.

ADAPTATION STAGE—REGULAR USE. In discussing some of the problems he thought involved in his addiction, Mr. N. said that there were many things happening inside him then. Briefly, these things may be summarized as confusion about body image; Mr. N. felt very uncomfortable in the "cage of self" and was not at all sure of his image as a man or a woman. He became tremendously preoccupied, even obsessed with this question, spending long hours before the mirror. He even drew a mustache on the mirror to appear older and more masculine. He was worried about his body, and wished he had hair on his chest and other kinds of proof that he was indeed a man. Being with the older boys and being accepted by them helped allay some of his anxiety. Looking back now, he can single out the first invitation through his brother, but the reasons for continuing with drugs were related to the complexes developed during puberty. He was a chubby boy, and this annoyed him because it was associated in his mind with femininity. He was also bothered greatly because he felt that he had a small penis. Furthermore, he felt his breast nipples were enlarged, and this, too, was a feminine trait. Drugs served admirably to cover his anxiety and depression around these complexes and to block out his obsessive doubts. Strangely, he said he looked at homosexuals, noted that some of them had muscles and no nipples, and he envied them. It is interesting that N. should have singled out homosexuals as objects of admiration or envy. He wished he had been created differently, not so chubby, and wondered why

God had not given him a body like that of these homosexuals. (Was he confusing homo- and heterosexual?) He went to extremes; he bought barbells and spent long hours trying to develop his musculature and physical appearance to a more masculine image.

At fifteen or sixteen, he began testing himself by going out with girls, but was never able to build close relationships. At first, he blamed drugs for this, but then saw that drugs were playing an important role in helping him avoid closeness and in finding "cop-out" reasons to avoid deeper relationships. He feared such closeness since he would need to expose his body and, inevitably, be rejected by the girls. He had sex only very infrequently in the next few years; "I can count the times on the fingers of one hand." If he went to bed with a girl, he had to put out the light and be sure he had an erection beforehand so that the girl would not notice what a small penis he had. He also developed feelings about gym and swimming because he would need to appear nude or take showers in front of other boys. Mr. N. was not too aware of these complexes or their meaning at the time—he simply blocked them out. If asked several years ago why he was using, he would have said he "liked it." It was not until 1959 that he first began analyzing and realizing he was using drugs to cope with many problems, mostly questions of body image, uncertainty, and adequacy. He found all kinds of reasons to dislike his body and brooded about all the different body parts at different times. Heroin served beautifully to allay these fears and increasingly replaced sex as a form of gratification. It entailed none of the hang-ups of sex, fears of closeness, or of being ridiculed, rejected by girls, or looked down on by boys. Drugs also helped him maintain his cool image; he could pretend to be as experienced and competent in sex as the other boys.

PHYSIOLOGICAL STAGE—ADDICTED. Another reason for using drugs was the fact that it became simpler to deal with only one problem—that of procuring and shooting drugs—instead of the manifold realities he found so difficult. However, he gradually began to become increasingly uncomfortable about using drugs, and this discomfort was exacerbated by the trauma inherent in his brother's dying in the Tombs while awaiting sentence. His brother experienced stomach pains while incarcerated, which the attendants attributed to withdrawal symptoms. When he complained, they beat him severely, and he was found dead the next morning. At this time, Mr. N. was away in Puerto Rico kicking his own habit. He was saddened by the death of his brother and felt lost, as if he had "lost his right arm." He managed to stay off a month after this and even got a job in a bank in Puerto Rico, but he slowly drifted back to using heroin.

Transition to Addiction System: Transitional Phase
Detoxification and Hospitalization

He now began going into hospitals and continued doing so for a number of years. He went to Lexington, Kentucky no less than seven times and also attempted withdrawal through the East Harlem Protestant Parish, Central Islip, Manhattan State, and Morris J. Bernstein Institute, as well as the Metropolitan and Riverside Hospitals. But he just couldn't make it. He thought the reason why hospitals didn't help was the fact that he really didn't want to stop at this time. He even began private therapy for seven months, but this too didn't help.

At one point, he went to a state hospital for treatment and was used as a "guinea pig." The hospital was conducting an experiment to find out whether a drug addict could withdraw himself if he were permitted to regulate the amount of drugs needed for withdrawal (this seems similar to the "monkey research" of self-administration of drugs conducted at Ann Arbor, Michigan, and Lexington, Kentucky). Mr. N. described a double bind situation at the hospital since his enclosure with psychotic patients was so upsetting that it became impossible for him to withdraw from drugs. There were many other factors impelling him to continue using, so the experiment was a failure from the beginning.

Transition to Abstinence

In retrospect, he realized that this hospitalization nevertheless marked a turning point for him. He saw it as miraculous that floridly psychotic patients who had flipped completely could change so dramatically with treatment. He realized that "human nature" is changeable and that if these "way-out" patients could make it, he could too.

Another crucial experience here was his meeting with another patient who later became his wife. She had been admitted because of suicidal attempts and also had as many complexes about sex as he. He was able to erase her complexes and she his, primarily through their acceptance of each other. In time, they were able to talk freely with each other, barring any secrets. Mr. N. expressed disillusionment with his therapist who did a "bad thing"; when he realized that Mr. N. and the girl were forming a relationship, he tried to separate them by divulging the confidences Mr. N. had revealed to him about his sexual and drug problems. The doctor probably thought he was doing a good thing, but this destroyed Mr. N.'s faith in psychiatry and therapy. On the other hand, he realized in retrospect that it was probably beneficial since he had been unable to tell his girl what his problems were. When she accepted them, he could accept and deal better with them himself, and this served to build their relationship. They discovered, in time, that they could be close, have a normal sexual relationship, and not be ridiculed or rejected.

EXPERIMENTATION STAGE—RECIDIVISM. When he left the hospital, Mr. N. continued to see her; she went out with him on a pass while she was still hospitalized. They were discovered, and further efforts were made to break it up. By this time, they were in love and nobody could stop it. Once outside, he again reverted to drugs. He began to use barbiturates to boost heroin and continued even more heavily to shoot Seconals. He thought the reason was that the treatment hadn't taken or because he had lost faith in the doctor. He became suicidal and wanted to do away with himself because he felt certain he could not succeed. In the past, every girl he had met had left him, and he now felt she would leave him, too. When she came out of the hospital, he tested her unbearably, trying to disillusion her to see if she could accept him in spite of his worst behavior. He was concerned about his own destructiveness in relation to her; he was bad for her, would never get off heroin, and would wind up hurting her as well. His main goal was to kill himself, and he experienced a number of O.D.'s on barbiturates and heroin. He became heavily habituated to Doridens, which he believes to be the worst pills. They were easier to obtain, and, while he began using them primarily as an "escape mechanism in a morbid sense," he enjoyed them since they were more effective than heroin in blocking out reality and making him blotto. He developed a weird ritual: shoot Seconals and pass out for a few seconds, then snap back and realize he was still alive. He would then open the Bible and stand near an open window, hoping for a miracle—that the wind would open the Bible page to a place where the word of God would be revealed. He found himself praying and pleading to God to help him and to give him enough strength— either to make it or to kill himself. He experienced a rush of religion at this point and tried to see whether the religious approach, as embodied in the Damascus Church in the Bronx or Teen Challenge in Brooklyn, could help him; but he walked out on both of them because he didn't feel they could.

ADAPTATIONAL STAGE—ABSTINENCE WITH SUPPORT. In 1965, his girl friend read some articles about Dr. Nyswander and the methadone maintenance research program and encouraged him to try it since she thought it would be the answer. Until then, he hadn't found any evidence that methadone worked, but he now discovered some of his former friends who looked as if they had just come out of a hospital or jail looking healthy, fat, and well-dressed. They told him they were making it on methadone on the street, and this convinced him. If it could work for them, it could work for him. Through a friend, he went to the Morris J. Bernstein Institute and was admitted into the program within a few weeks.

At the time, he still had doubts about making it. Something his girl friend said to him at the time crystallized his resolution: "Do you want to make it, or do you want to want to make it?" He probed into himself and answered that he really wanted to make it. He believed it was a fifty-fifty proposition: if methadone could help him with 50 percent, he would be responsible for the other 50 percent. He was able to make it because his girl friend loved and believed in him, and helped him overcome his complexes. He could now see a way out, whereas he had been unable to find any exit before. His doctor at the time advised him not to marry for awhile, and he waited seven months before he did so. He needed to be on welfare for awhile, but then began to work as a research aide in the program. He only "goofed" once at the beginning when he took heroin while an inpatient. Luckily, this was not discovered, and he has not goofed since, aside from occasional pot smoking. He has a very good record in the program and is proud that he has been off for three years now.

Tolerance of Abstinence

Regarding the question of getting off methadone as well, he said he has mixed feelings about this. He would, indeed, like to get off some day since he feels that the best way is complete abstinence. Other people in the program do not subscribe to this view, however. He sometimes views it as a simple matter of arithmetic; that is, he was a drug addict for sixteen years and on methadone only three, and it still doesn't balance out. What prevents him from using now is that drugs don't appeal to him any longer because he has found a new "high," that of being normal and getting normal gratifications. "99 percent of the time" he doesn't experience any craving, but if an urge should occur for a few minutes, he is able to cope with it, and it disappears.

In discussing his primary family, which I pointed out he had blocked out in his discussion, he thought his mother contributed to his addiction unknowingly. Although he covered this up, it was apparent that a double-bind relationship existed, that she unconsciously fed him mixed messages, and was seductive. He pointed out, for example, that after his brother's death, she left five dollars around for him each morning, knowing that he would use it to get off on drugs. He justified this on the basis of her fear that he might get arrested, wind up in jail, and die like his brother before him. There was evidence of overprotectiveness and a covering up for him in relation to the father as well. The parents were both ignorant of drugs and unable to cope when they learned about their sons' use. They reacted with anger and sadness, and the father, at times, beat both boys. Mr. N. recalls that the father once said, "Let me go and try it so I'll see what you find in it." The mother had, before this, consistently blocked out any knowledge of their drug use, although all the signs were right under her nose. Mr. N. said he felt especially related to the father and was the father's favorite, while the brother was his mother's favorite. The father was a rather strong person who worked in an unskilled factory occupation. He drank a great deal and could be termed a semi- or complete alcoholic, although he could stop himself. His nerves were not always up to par as a result. Mr. N. said there was no way of generalizing about how anybody becomes a drug addict; it's very individual. There was no way of telling how anyone gets off of drugs, as well, since this, too, is unique and individual.

Discussion

The family constellation for Mr. N., a Puerto Rican, appears not too different from that observed with other ethnic groups, in fact it closely approximates the classic picture described for families of addicts: a seductive and overprotective mother who involves the son in a double-bind situation, feeding him hidden destructive messages. There is evidence also of "emotional divorce" between the parents, each singling off and choosing a child as his or her favorite. The family situation differs somewhat in that Mr. N. sees himself as being closer to the father than the mother. What is fairly typical or, at least frequent, is the existence of an alcoholic father who serves as a prototype for drug abuse or impulsive living. Somewhat more unusual, although not at all uncommon, is the existence of two boys on drugs in one family. The brother appears to have been seductive in leading Mr. N. first to gang fighting and then to drugs (there are sexual or homosexual overtones in Mr. N.'s first encounter with the brother's drug use), and the brother served as an important role model for Mr. N. His death helped precipitate a desire to change.

Not at all unusual is the beginning reversal of values and drug experimentation about the time of puberty. The onset of pubescence obviously reinforced many of Mr. N.'s doubts about his adequacy as a man and psychosexual confusion. He seems to have been obsessed with numerous problems of body image and was never comfortable within himself, constantly struggling with fears of femininity and homosexuality. Drugs served admirably to block out these doubts and to cop out of close relationships and sexuality; in time they became the preferred means of gratification since he didn't need to expose himself to ridicule and rejection.

The cool image became an important social reinforcement, augmenting his feeling of ego mastery and helping him define his social role and behavior. He assumed the rituals and mannerisms for being cool and could even feel superior to the squares. By being an addict, he needed only to cope with one problem rather than a plethora.

As he got further into drugs, his self-hatred was increasingly mobilized in the form of self-destructive impulses, hopelessness and O.D.'s. Two aspects of his hospitalization emerge as most important in his later making it: seeing floridly psychotic patients become well helped him believe that it could also happen to him; and by forming a relationship, sharing his deepest fears, and being accepted by a woman, he could then accept himself and begin to emerge from the drug scene. This point is worth remembering in any program evaluation: the results of a treatment program may not become apparent until years later and may be attributed to the latest treatment modality.

CASE OF MR. N.   PENTECOSTAL

Brotman-Freedman Typology
1. Normal conventionality   —
2. Criminality and hustling   —
3. Family conventionality   —
4. Friend conventionality   —
Classification: "Hustler"

Chein's Typology
Combination of emulation of brother, desire to achieve "cool" image and belong. He also needed to relieve deeply rooted tensions and anxiety occasioned by fears of femininity and homosexuality, concern about a "defective" body image, etc.

Life Cycle
Street addict.

Social Milieu
Returned to neighborhood from hospitals, jail, Puerto Rico.

Cloward-Ohlin
Retreatist in sense surrendered square values, stopped being a "good boy" in order to become "cool" like his brother.

Case of Family G.

Mrs. G., a slight, dark-complected woman with a decided Puerto Rican accent, stated that she was forty-one years old, but appeared older. Her hands were criss-crossed with scars, and she attributed this to her inability to tolerate the quinine in the heroin she used so many years. She sniffed for a long time and demonstrated that she could pass a matchstick through the septum of her nose because a hole resulted from her sniffing. She didn't appear at all hostile to the "white establishment," and, in fact, spoke well of the various doctors who treated her at the Lexington Hospital and in the methadone program.

Addiction Set—Predisposing Social and Psychological Factors

Mrs. G. at first attributed her addiction to "environment" and to friends she hung out with in the deprived areas of New York City. However, as she continued, she described various psychological problems emanating from childhood. She wept at points during the interview; much of this related to continued feelings of loss over the death of her father and, subsequently, of the paternal grandfather, which had reactivated feelings about her father. Another area where she evidenced strong concern was her children. "They were mine, the only thing I had."

Her father, a Puerto Rican, died when she was only six. She had been very close to him, and "a part of me died with him." She frequently wonders why he had to die and is sure her life would have been different if he hadn't died so young. Her mother took care of her, but she never had any real love from her in comparison with the smothering she received from the father. When the mother remarried a year and a half later, she resented the stepfather and was sent to New York to live with a very strict uncle and more tolerant grandmother. She was "cooped up" and unable to enjoy freedom like other girls. By fifteen, she was attending school two days a week and working in a factory. The uncle forged her working papers, and she needed to hide in the bathroom of the factory whenever inspectors came around. From working at such a young age, she learned to be independent. The uncle didn't let her finish school because he claimed he couldn't support her. When the grandmother died, she ran away and stayed with an older woman who befriended her. The uncle had a warrant issued and she was committed to a wayward minor's home at the age of fifteen. She remained there a year and remembers it as a terrible experience.

She recalled that she was introverted, quiet, and a "loner" at this time. She denied that there were problems of transition from Puerto Rico to America, saying that she was adaptable and picked up languages easily. She developed bitter feelings as she looked back at her life: she had been crazy about her father and had everything when he was alive; then she was deprived of his presence and even lost her mother, who married another man and had children while she needed to come to New York. She suffered with the strict uncle and saw her grandmother die finally.

Tolerance for Potential Addiction—Initiation to Drug Use

She was made a ward of the woman-friend and enjoyed more freedom than before. She started using pot, and through this met her husband, who was one year older than she. She thought her husband was very similar to herself; he too had been on his own since twelve or thirteen, although he had an intact family. She was unable to explain her new associations with people who were "freer," simply saying these were the people she was thrown in with. She admitted being uncomfortable with them if she was observed by adults. If ordinary square people invited her to visit, she shied away. Her uncle died a few months after she left the home, and she was now alone in the city and her own boss. She felt anger towards the uncle, who had not only had her committed, but indicated in his warrant that she was no longer a virgin, when in fact she was.

She described her husband as "not the best, and not the

worst." He had had a rough life and his problems had a lot to do with his childhood. At eighteen, he was busted for pot and sent to jail so that she was again on her own. She lost her job, and a girl friend told her about "easy money" by sleeping with men. Since she owed rent, she did it; but emphasized that it was only for the money and that she was really not cut out for that kind of life. When her husband returned from jail, she moved in with him again and became pregnant and had her first child, a boy. She said she always "loved kids and animals." Her husband was not too responsible so that she had to resume her activities with men. The husband knew about her prostitution, but did nothing to stop her because they needed the money. He was becoming increasingly involved with heroin, but she did not know it at the time. She found work as a salesgirl and sent for her sister from Puerto Rico to care for the child while she worked. Her husband obtained his seaman's papers and was able to ship out, using this as a means of controlling his heroin habit. She was again pregnant and was delivered of a second son.

Things became difficult at this time because her mother had left the stepfather and came to live with them with four children by the stepfather. She also had her sister living with her. Her husband was "dipping and dabbing" in heroin, although she claimed she still did not know it then. In terms of "work," her husband began to do well because he was running numbers and earning forty cents on every dollar. Her mother was unable to get on welfare because she didn't meet the two years' residence requirement, and her husband supported her as well. Money soon began to run short and Mrs. G. again resorted to her male "friends." Her prostitution (she didn't use this word herself) didn't bother her too much because she felt she was helping her stepbrothers and liked doing it for the mother. She assumes the mother knew about it since she wasn't "dumb." Her husband was picked up for numbers several times and finally decided to return to the ship.

Mrs. G. emphasized that she would have liked a different kind of life and always held on to her square ideals, such as being a housewife or a nurse, or helping others since she was good with children. Her husband was similarly interested in helping people and would have liked to work as a counselor in a program. They were able to find the mother a separate apartment in the building, which relieved the overcrowding. Mrs. G. again became pregnant with her youngest child, a girl. She began to notice that her husband woke up sick every morning, yet felt better shortly after some friends visited him while she was busy preparing coffee. She was very sick herself during this last pregnancy and had, in fact, been troubled by different conditions: a "touch of asthma" and, more serious, troubles with her esophagus, which had shrunk and was frequently closed off. A female friend of her husband's, who was a hustler and drug user, came to the house and, when she learned that Mrs. G. was not feeling well, suggested that she take some "coke." Actually it was heroin mixed with cocaine, though Mrs. G. didn't know it, and used it whenever she felt unwell. She couldn't now explain how she became more and more involved with heroin, but at the beginning it was mainly the fact that the pain subsided whenever she used this concoction. When she found out about her husband's heroin use, she was upset and angry. Her husband denied that he kept it in the house, and said he had tried to keep things separate by doing it on the street to keep her uninvolved. She herself was chipping, but thought it was coke, as indicated. She developed strange symptoms and a friend finally told her she was hooked. She didn't know what this meant and had it explained to her. She thought she had been "lucky" because she was able to obtain drugs very cheaply by the spoonful without difficulty. When her husband learned about her addiction, he was furious and beat her, blaming himself for it. He took her to various doctors to get off, and she began using Dolophine, gradually mixing it with heroin again.

Adaptational Stage—Regular Use

Her husband was again "busted" in 1954 and sentenced to a state prison. She became hooked again. At this time, her paternal grandfather, of whom she was very fond, was living with her and taking care of the rent. Her husband wanted her to leave the children with his mother in New Jersey while she went to a hospital, but she was reluctant to do so. She was unhappy, also, because the older boy had learned of her addiction and resented it. She didn't know how to get off and felt increasingly uncomfortable with her asthma, esophagus condition, and what she learned was an ulcer, as well. She spent five days at Bellevue because she was run down and terribly underweight. She had a rough time with welfare, which refused to help her, claiming that her parents were responsible for her. Her husband came out of jail a year and a half later, and her "friends" needed to to help her during this time. She was reluctant to call them "tricks" or "Johns," and was grateful to them because they were like substitute husbands, giving her money whenever she needed it and even helping out at Christmas for the children. Drug addiction or not, her children never had to do without things. In fact, she felt she spoiled them by giving them too much in the form of love and material things. All the boys were interested in sports, and the youngest one had aspirations to become a great athlete. They won trophies, and she is proud of them all. When her husband came home, he returned to work, but did not earn very much, and the grandfather continued to pay the rent. She developed a complex about her drug use and avoided her neighbors.

Her husband remained clean for six months and worked, but soon became disgusted because he wasn't earning enough. She was hooked on Dolophines and the heroin she copped. She rationalized that it was hard to go to a doctor and wait for the Dolophines; it was much easier to cop and avoid bothering with a doctor. She finally began to receive help from welfare, but needed to claim that her husband was not in the home. The money from welfare was "like from heaven" since it helped her over the rough spots. She felt bad about taking money from the grandfather; he was old and he shouldn't be doing the job of her husband.

Her husband was now framed by the police, who planted a set of works on him because they had been watching him. Her husband had always protected her in his selling activities, giving her supplies and making sure she was never exposed to the rough parts of drug addiction. In fact, he conducted the selling like a regular business and dealt only with choice customers. They both budgeted themselves carefully to make sure they kept their supply constant and didn't run short. They were careful with their main connection, too, again as part of their good business approach.

Still later, their main connection was busted and her husband warned her that he was now working for the "Feds" and that she should be leery of him. A "friend" of this connection kept pestering her to cop drugs for him, and she finally gave in, though suspecting he was trying to entrap her. For this, she got five years, and her husband was pulled in for a similar term under the Jones "Conspiracy Act," in 1962. Her husband was upset by her conviction and tried to get her out of it, but it was impossible. Mrs. G. wept at this point because her grandfather and her mother now learned about her addiction, and she felt exposed and ashamed. She and her husband were committed to Lexington and spent forty months there. She thought a lot of good had come out of this stay, but there were bad aspects, too, in terms of her neglect of the children. Her mother took them in because they preferred to be with her. Leaving the children hurt her most; but she also cried now because she had never had a chance to make it up to the grandfather who had done so much for her and who died while she was at Lexington.

She liked the doctors at Lexington and was glad to learn from them that she was "not like the average addict." She also learned to assert herself more instead of being a "soft touch." (Comments from some of the counselors in the methadone program are that Mrs. G. is quite a controling person, and this was part of the problem with the middle child.) While at Lexington, her oldest boy volunteered for the service and made a generally good career for himself in the Army. It was the middle child who fared the worst since he engaged in truancy and was eventually sent to a state training school.

Though she had had a rough time in her life, Mrs. G. felt that "God and the good angels" looked out for her. She managed to keep her camouflage, on the whole, and was never fully exposed or roughed it as other addicts do. She added some of her own aphorisms such as, "It isn't *what* you do, but *how* you do it"—in other words, the *style* is important. Another favorite saying, which was repeated several times, was "You don't shit where you eat," by which she meant that she tried to keep her drug life and home life separate. The boy was the severest trial for her, especially when she learned he was involved with drugs.

Tolerance for Potential Abstinence—Experimental Stage—Recidivism

Both she and her husband came out of Lexington in 1964 and were placed on twenty months' "conditional release." They managed to stay off during this time, but reverted as soon as this period was over. They found the boy hooked when they came home. Mrs. G. went the rounds of doctors to get Dolophine pills for the boy. She said she wouldn't blame the boy for her own relapse, but she proved weak and again began to use drugs. Her husband began selling to survive since jobs were hard to find. In the summer of 1967, her boy was busted, and in December 1967 committed to a hospital under the NACC civil-commitment program.

She and her husband applied for the methadone maintenance program, which was just being established but needed to wait several years more to get in. They were exhausted by the drug life, and Mrs. G. finally wrote to the hospital administration telling about her son and indicating they had been waiting a long time to be admitted. They received a prompt response and were admitted to a program in Brooklyn.

They had trouble adjusting to the program at first. Mr. G. continued selling drugs because he felt he owed his customers something and shouldn't cut them loose abruptly. He finally gave them all the heroin he had and warned them that he was stopping, which he did. Both she and her husband continued to shoot and "cheat" with drugs until they realized they must cut the whole scene loose. Her husband was tired of jails after spending long periods away from home, including three years of a larger sentence at Lexington. Mrs. G. was honest with the doctors in the program and didn't attempt to conceal her use

during this time. They were both sure that methadone was a
way out, and this has in fact proven to be true.

They reached their final solution when she said, "If you stop,
I'll stop." He replied, "I don't twist your arm to use, and if you're
cheating, you must take responsibility for it yourself." This
stuck with her. She remembers that she was lying down at this
time and suddenly said to herself, "This is the truth. If I stop,
he will stop too." The thought bothered her for a few days.
At this time, her husband was using the methadone, but also
taking a shot each morning. Suddenly, they both felt better on
the methadone and decided they must give it a chance. Her
husband broke all of his needles in her presence, but she was
not impressed since he could get more elsewhere. She nevertheless said nothing, but then noticed that her husband was no
longer taking his morning shot. This happened about Christmas
or New Year's and probably represented part of their joint
decision to stop. Since then, there have been no more drugs
and no selling.

She thought her husband was a quiet man who had a wall
around him, and the drugs served to keep him functioning. He
lost his job as a maintenance man but then found another as a
driver. After they did better, her son also began to improve
in the program; and he too hasn't touched drugs since. Mrs. G.
prided herself on the fact that he never stole from their home.
She was hurt that he avoided her when she used drugs. He is
now living with a girl and has a child by her. Like his parents,
he is interested in finding a job as a counselor in a methadone
program. The youngest child, who was always rather stubborn
and assertive, according to Mrs. G., is training to be a stenog-
rapher and will probably make a career of this. Mrs. G. is
working, but would like to become a counselor in a methadone
program and implied she would welcome my help with this.
She was proud that she and her husband could now buy a car
and get about easily. She feels good about the boys and believes
that life will now offer them the things denied them all these
years. In time, she would like to get off methadone maintenance
as well, but she will cross that bridge when she comes to it.

CASE OF FAMILY G. METHADONE MAINTENANCE

Brotman-Freedman Typology
1. Normal conventionality ?
2. Criminal history —
3. Family conventionality ?
4. Friend conventionality ?

(dealing, numbers, and prostitution)
(mixed picture)

> Classification: Mrs. "Hustler-conformist?" (two-worlder); Mr. Dealer in numbers, also "two-worlder."

Chein's Typology

Looking for father figure and felt alone and unloved. Curious combination of conventional family living with association with husband who was a drug addict. Hustled to get money. Saw nothing wrong in many of the "deviant" things she was doing. "It isn't the things you do, it's the way you do it." Son emulated the parents and became an addict.

Life Cycle

Family situation deteriorating when addiction was revealed to relatives. Went to Lexington and saw son become an addict.

Social Milieu

Puerto Rico to America to Lexington to New York.

Cloward-Ohlin

No clear relationship here—not truly retreatist—has conventional goals for self and family.

NO PROGRAM—MADE IT ON OWN

Case of Mr. S.

This thirty-eight-year-old man appeared as a bright and alert individual, proud of his cleverness and of being one step ahead of others. He was extremely circumstantial in his account of how he became an addict and grew out of his addiction. He compulsively included every detail so that the "interview" became very extended, in fact lasting almost a day and a half.

Tolerance for Addiction

BEGINNING ADDICTION SET—SOCIAL AND FAMILIAL BACKGROUND. Mr. S. traced the beginnings of his drug addiction to his tenth

year. He recently began looking back that far to find out why
he began to get into trouble. If it hadn't been drugs, it would
have been something else; his "character disorder" was already
forming then. (The term "character disorder" stemmed from
his association with the therapeutic community which uses this
diagnosis for all its residents.) It was about this time that he began
picking up things that didn't belong to him and he knew it was
wrong. Although he knew the "right way," he continued doing it,
manipulating and planning to get his own way.

He came from a large family that included six girls and eight
boys. He was the youngest of the boys and the only one who
became an addict except for a sister whom he later helped get
off drugs. Interestingly, he failed to mention another sister who
also became addicted and has never been able to get off. There
were five older females. The father was an alcoholic, distant and
undemonstrative, yet stern and proud. He came from the
Caribbean and behaved like a "true British subject," laying down
very rigid rules of behavior which allowed for no deviation. The
father maintained his dignity and never hung around bars, drinking at home and, in fact, making his own liquor. He drank
steadily and worked in Philadelphia, where the family spent most
of their life. He never allowed any fun in the house and was "a
hell of a disciplinarian" of the old Victorian school. He didn't
even allow whistling in the home, and things were even worse
on Sundays. He was especially strict with the girls. In a freer
moment, Mr. S. described the father as "weird."

From the beginning, he was involved in testing the father.
At one point, he actually stole the father's "special Viennese
bread," knowing this would invite punishment, which indeed
followed. Actually, his brother egged him on to provoke the
father; Mr. S. tried to show his boldness by saying he would hit
the father with a hammer if the father annoyed him. In fact, he
acted quite ignominiously and hid under the bed, whence his
father dragged him out and beat him. The mother was hard-
working, took very good care of him and had plenty of love
for him. A very strong motif in all of Mr. S.'s behavior appeared
to be a constant testing of her to see whether she would stay

with him no matter what he did. Another element was that Mr. S. saw himself as, or behaved like, two persons, one superficially good, the other bad, so that the two images or worlds never met. Home was a place to be good, and outside the place to be bad, and it was important to keep them separate. These two images reappear regularly in his later life, in the service and elsewhere. He continuously defied and subverted the father's rules while testing the mother to remain with him no matter what he did.

Another important element in his life was the feeling that he was always losing out in comparison with his brothers. While being younger had advantages in that the parents were tired by the time he was born and no longer as strict as with the older boys (who all conformed and made it in legitimate ways), he always felt underprivileged and abandoned. An older sister took him in tow for awhile when he was nine and brought him to girls' classes, so that he was, in fact, associating more with girls at this time than with boys. He claimed he was unable to make male friends because of his youth, but also because he had no money to get to the boys' community centers.

A recurring grievance in his youth was the fact that he could not get to a summer camp, which represented a dream of beauty to him. In various ways he later tried to compensate for this deprivation by playing hooky from school and by enlisting. The elements of feeling left out and being too young to qualify were important motifs in his life. The brothers could always get to community centers and summer camps, for example, because they could work at the centers, and camps were glad to have them. He recalls one summer when all the brothers went off to camp and he was left alone feeling desolate.

In response to the question of why he developed a tolerance for doing wrong and choosing wrong knowing right, he said that, although he went wrong, the guidelines were fixed, and he was always aware of them even in his wrong-doing. He thought it especially inexcusable that he should do wrong knowing that there were rules to which he should conform and that violating them led inevitably to hell. Still, he never hesitated and was increasingly sucked into the bad way, which eventually led to drug use, though at the rather late age of twenty-four. One important factor in his life was that he was rebelling because he wasn't able to do what he wanted and reached a point in life where he was fighting for his independence. He resented being denied privileges such as playing cards or going out. The house was a prison. If the father or mother could not watch him, they relegated the responsibility to the older boys and girls, and he was beaten if he didn't obey. He could never smoke in the house and, even at twenty-five, felt peculiar smoking in front of his mother. He was so busy acting out without thinking that it was only during the periods of arrest, which occurred after he was fifteen, that he had a chance to take stock and think about what was happening. He was divided against himself since many of the things he was doing were against "my whole way of thinking," and he was in conflict. He knew better decisions needed to be made, but somehow he could never make them, nor muster any willpower, and he rationalized his doubts away. He kept sinking, and this made him feel even worse. This came later, however, since he revelled for a long time in what he was doing, and the kicks greatly outweighed his scruples.

His family saw him as a goody-goody. He brought out the differences between his superficial appearance and his actual feelings and behavior. For a long time, he was trusted with important errands, even during blizzards, because everyone knew he was smart and could find his way back. He also worked hard, seven days a week, shining shoes and doing other things to earn the money his family could not provide. Then a sudden transformation occurred; he himself doesn't understand how or why, but he thinks now that it was very queer. At the beginning, he simply acted up in school or stole things, but did not take to drugs. In fact, he was able to resist drugs although his friends were fooling around with liquor and pills. He had had a painful experience at the age of seven when he stole the wine his father made at home and became drunk. He acted "crazy," and his sister beat him with an umbrella. He was ridiculed by the entire family so that he hesitated to try liquor again. When he later took to drugs, it came as a great surprise to the family.

Although he had been very good in school, he suddenly began acting up and following the lead of a friend, who was a rebel and instigated other students against the teachers. He felt that his difficulties in school were precipitated by the fact that one of the teachers was very stern and seemed to know the "real character" of Mr. S. He continued this behavior until he was failed for conduct (not for his intelligence, which he took care to stress as very important to him). Although he assumed a facade of not caring, he cried "uncontrollably" when he came home because it was a terrible thing to fail in Philadelphia. Another factor was his playing hooky, which tied in with his continuing desire for a vacation and summer camp experience. If he couldn't get to camp, he would at least play hooky and swim and break the rules, and he did this increasingly. After a while, his resentment was crystallized against the school, and he began to fail in his academic subjects, whereas it had previously been for conduct alone.

He began hanging around with undesirable kids, playing hooky, stealing, and rifling lockers. He and his friends gravitated towards department stores and five-and-tens like a "gang of thieves." Whereas the other kids ended up in reform schools, he managed to pull out in time; either fortune was looking out for him or he was smarter and could get away with things. Many of the boys who used drugs with him later died, and he was one of the very few to survive. The things he stole were not all useful; he enjoyed taking things just for the kick of stealing and outsmarting somebody. Still, even in his stealing there were certain things he would not do, such as snatch purses from old ladies. Whenever he was tempted to do this, he thought of his mother; the idea of hitting a woman and grabbing her purse proved beyond him. He was also reluctant to steal from the poor since it brought home the situation of his own family. He could not engage in violence although there had been gang-bopping fights over area boundaries and "turf." He enjoyed outwitting his teachers as well as his father, who was always checking up on him. He realized now that he was playing a game with life and was not honest with himself.

Still, if something hadn't happened to him, or if the teachers hadn't gotten him, "Mother Nature" would have, because he was a "product of nature." He had a pretty good idea that things were going to catch up with him and how it would end, but this did not deter him. He felt good because there were secondary gains such as recognition from others and pride in his ability to manipulate things toward his own ends to keep people from pushing him around. He also liked being smart enough to control two different worlds, the good and the bad. In addition he had something else: he had been born with two extra fingers— an extra pinkey on each hand, and he used these to frighten kids when they picked on him. He felt that he had a special power and could use it to keep the bullies off. One finger was very tiny and his mother removed it one night with a horsehair. The other one was removed while in jail for the last time in 1960. But at thirteen, he was still busy living it up. His horizons had expanded since he no longer hung out with the local group, but was associating with bad boys from other sections of the city and engaging in raids and depredations on local department stores.

EXPERIMENTATION AND ADAPTATIVE USE. At sixteen, he began fooling around with different things, grass and pills. At this time, his gang all became anxious to join the Summer Reserve, primarily as a means of getting away to a summer camp. Mr. S.'s brother was already in the Army, and he felt envious. He lied about his age and joined up. With this act, he thought he had entered a good phase again, but this was questionable since he continued his "bad career" in service, extending his deviant activities to black marketing and drug use. He was happy to enlist, since four brothers had served in the Army in World War II, and some were in service subsequently. He was the only male left at home, too young to be included; and he felt himself not a man as a result—always missing out. The brothers travelled about in the big world and did exciting things, but not he.

He therefore enlisted and spent two weeks on maneuvers with the Reserve. He lived intensively and hardly slept this entire period, keeping himself going with bennies—actually the cotton from nasal inhalators which he chewed. He discovered that it not only kept him awake, but also made him talkative which he relished, apparently having been less articulate before. It gave him energy, and he then took more to combat the "down" feeling and depression which followed. He added marijuana and wine since he found they went well together.

The Korean War broke out at this time and he remained with the Reserve Unit, which was activated. He then "cast all fate to the winds." He had an omnipotent feeling that he could handle any situation and any drugs. At this time, he met up with a fast theatre crowd while temporarily visiting New York. He was proud that he was the only one accepted by them. They introduced him to cocaine and showed him how to snort it by spreading it on a mirror and sniffing it up through straws in their nostrils. He pretended he already knew about cocaine.

In service, he associated with the same group of neighborhood boys. Time began to hang heavy on their hands, and he organized a system for getting drugs which he is still proud of. The men pooled their money and sent an emissary through a railroad porter connection to bring back pot. Unknown to him, this emissary also brought back heroin for some of the other men. They were all part of an in-group and were looked up to enviously by the outsiders. Mr. S. spent time explaining his cleverness in organizing a business in service—selling sandwiches and drinks and employing a field kitchen, a jeep, and a number of enlisted men. He was the prime mover here, proud of his ability to persuade officers to look the other way, provided he gave them their sandwiches free. He also "shylocked" and was so bold as to wait beside the paymaster when the checks were being handed out to the men so that he could be the first to collect his debts. He was smoking pot and using more ups and downs.

In 1956, the unit was shifted abroad. Mr. S. had earned a large sum of money gambling on board the ship going there, and he now invested heavily in black market activities. He travelled over different parts of Europe with a limited knowledge of language, yet managed to meet the criminal elements and deal with them. He was again leading a double life since he was engaging in illegal activities and also seeing prostitutes when he needed sex. At the same time, he managed to seek out respectable but poor families who would have been horrified if they knew about his other activities. He spent his weekends with these families in the country and brought them all kinds of gifts for which he never charged them. He disliked associating with criminal elements and only remained with them long enough to conclude his business.

TOLERANCE FOR ADDICTION. This continued until 1958 when he returned to the United States and was discharged honorably. Before his discharge, he had begun to experiment with heroin and found it "fascinating." There was something about it—it made him sick and nauseous; still, after throwing up, a very special feeling remained in that he felt very high, light-headed, and he could feel that "this was the way out."

He had a large sum of money on his hands together with his mustering-out pay; he wondered how best to invest it in some new enterprise. He decided to "deal in weight," i.e. sell drugs. He began this but never expected to get hooked himself and get so irretrievably caught up in drug use. He took no chances, using an intermediary to buy his drugs for him. For a long time, he continued snorting. He was living in Philadelphia; the family had moved to New York after the father died while he was in camp, and it hit him hard. The circumstances under which he first realized he was hooked were interesting, yet typical for him. He was preparing to work for the post office and was seeing a girl of good family, while using prostitutes for sex. He was supposed to take the girl to the circus, so he needed to stay with her for about twelve hours. His nose began running, and the girl pointed it out to him. He began to "fall out" and couldn't even tie his shoelaces. His cigarettes tasted bad, and he wondered if this was it, but hoped it was only a cold. When he finally delivered the girl home, he felt so weak he rushed over to a friend. When he snorted again, all his symptoms disappeared. He realized he was hooked and "it couldn't get worse," but he blocked it out. As his money disappeared, he realized he couldn't afford to snort any longer. He asked a friend to hit his arm with a needle, and he began mainlining. Even here, he needed to emphasize his unusual powers: he insisted the friend hit him with as large an amount of drugs as he had been snorting. "I could have died, but my resistance was strong."

This continued "on and on" until he was busted by a police agent. They were cleaning up Philadelphia at the time, and he and his friends were rounded up and jailed. Here too, he needed to show his stamina: he hid his withdrawal symptoms to prove he was not an addict, not knowing that they had the goods on him anyhow since he had unwittingly sold heroin to an agent. It was hell withdrawing, and he stayed in jail several months. It was at this time that his family first discovered he was using heroin. He was committed to the Public Health Hospital at Lexington, Kentucky. While there, he learned a good deal about drugs, which he later used to make connections in New York where he moved from Philadelphia. While hospitalized, he began taking on a "different" personality which was "more positive." He had a chance to think and read, which he enjoyed. He was able to learn a great deal about narcotic addiction, and, for the first time, became aware that personality problems were involved. He also had some sessions with a psychiatrist. He was proud of the psychiatrist's progress report, which indicated that Mr. S. would never return to Lexington. For the first time, he began to realize that drugs destroyed a person, and he wondered why he would want to continue something which was going to destroy him. He especially enjoyed Norman Vincent Peale's *Power of Positive Thinking* since it was so clear and simple and taught him how to concentrate, go to sleep, and generally improve himself. He didn't understand what he was escaping, but he felt his reading prepared him for his later abstinence, even though it didn't stop him from relapsing to drugs as soon as he got out.

In fact, he now became a junkie of the first order and continued selling drugs. He was again arrested when they found the works and dope on him. The judge who condemned him turned out to be his former Army officer. He felt bad about being found out. He had reached a very low point since he was ready to take anything to block out reality and gain oblivion.

In fact, his friends brought all kinds of drugs to him to test, and he didn't care what he did to himself; he was ready to use anything without concern about the consequences.

It was at this point that things became so hot for him in Philadelphia. Everyone seemed to know him and to be watching his every move, especially two friends of his cousin who were detectives and appeared all the time to catch him. He therefore decided to leave Philadelphia, packed all his clothes, and took forty decks of heroin with him to New York. By this time, he had lost all his "principles," and was prepared to do anything to survive in the heroin world. He realized he was sinking step by step, and he didn't know how low he would go. He moved into the home of his mother, who knew about his drug use. He thought it interesting that she should risk ostracism from her brothers to whom she was very attached, rather than abandon him, and he was proud that she stood by him. She had visited him when he was arrested in Philadelphia, and his sister, who had begun fooling around with drugs, came with her. In New York, he felt strange because he had no connections, and the forty bags, as well as the money, went awfully fast. Still, he was sick and needed to cop; he therefore began frequenting the haunts around Lexington Avenue, pawning his mother's clothing, and stealing everything in the house, even the sheets and the toys of the nephews.

The worst came when he began stealing from a purse his mother kept hidden in her bed. This held about seven hundred dollars, and he took small amounts, about twenty dollars at a time, preying on his mother, lying around in wait for her to move out of the room. He even pressured the mother directly for money because he was sick. For the first time, he began to "feel pain" from the drugs. The pain began to hit him in the legs and in the stomach as if they were tied in a knot. His will-power could no longer help him, and he found himself moaning, but he got no consolation from the sister, who simply laughed. He no longer cared, however, and when the mother refused to give him two dollars for a shot, he stole his nephew's coat and pawned it. He was, in fact, hoping he would be arrested, and when the sister threatened to do it, he wanted her to carry it through, but she couldn't. The next day, the mother told him to get out of the house because he had stolen the sheets. This hit him hard and he left.

As part of this separation, he learned new ways to get money since he could no longer steal from the home. He therefore began shoplifting and hit on the idea of stealing seafood since this brought the best returns. He also arranged for contacts in beauty and barber shops where he sold the stuff. He laughed as he remembered that there was a great demand for his products, and he could hardly keep up with it. At the same time, he wasn't doing too well since he was increasingly being arrested for shoplifting and was actually in jail five times in the short period of two months. He was finally fingerprinted and sent to jail for ninety days. When he came out, his mother was there as usual. She took him in and gave him money for a job, which he used for drugs instead. He was soon readdicted, once more began stealing from the home, and pawned his mother's new radio. He now began sleeping in cellars, which he hated, and developed pustular fungus sores all over the body. Although he had formerly been very neat about his appearance and about bathing, he no longer cared; he went downhill and did all the things he had previously loathed. He slept in rat-infested cellars that frequently drained human refuse when the toilets over-flowed. An endless round ensued of being arrested, going to the workhouse, then coming back to the cellars, stealing, and using drugs; and this cycle continued endlessly. The funny thing was that the mother took him back every time he approached her.

He slept in filthy basements in this way for three years and became inured to the smell, which would have stifled other people. He became an outcast even among the junkies, who could not understand how he could live this way and described him as "disgusting." They were surprised that he could survive at all through all the coal fumes, the back-drainage, and revolting conditions of the cellar. He slept on piles of coal and no longer cared what he did; he was conditioned to the cellar. He could never stand rats and centipedes before, but was now surrounded by them and could feel them all over his body. His whole way of thinking had deteriorated. Normally, he had a strong desire for sex, but now drugs replaced everything, and he could even sleep in the same bed with a girl and not be interested. He caught lice from a wino, who slept next to him, and he needed to be deloused when he went to jail. He was picked up for shoplifting, but was at times able to outwit the detectives and talk them out of putting him in jail. He could still be proud of this achievement.

TOLERANCE FOR ABSTINENCE. He was terribly upset when he returned from one of his jail sentences to learn that his sister had been burned to death. He had felt very close to her, and the shock of reality was very painful. He was crying and sincere in his profession not to go back to drugs, but this didn't stop him. It nevertheless marked a turning point for him because he associated the sister's death with his mother. He felt that he would be in jail one day and the mother would die while he was away, and he would really and finally be alone in the world with no way out. He felt terribly lonely at this time since he believed the family had cut all ties with him, and he vowed not to steal from the mother again.

It was under all the pressures, after having hit rock bottom, that his craving for drugs suddenly took a strange turn and he began considering the possibility of being able to get off drugs and function without it. He thought it was the double shock of the sister's death and his mother turning away from him which helped precipitate the change. Also, whatever adaptational values adhered to his being bad and rebelling were no longer holding up, and the life of addiction was becoming increasingly intolerable. The one sustaining factor was his mother, and to a lesser degree, his sister, who still wanted to help him. But he felt that, too, would come to an end now, and he would really be alone finally. He had to do something to help himself and prove himself to them. After a while, he began noting that his craving was "mostly in the mind," and some of the physical aspects had changed. He began experimenting by not using over a weekend and found that this no longer represented a problem.

Things finally came to a head when, in order to get money for drugs, he participated indirectly in a burglary with other addicts. To some extent, he absolved himself, claiming that he had simply gone in to look around and see if the coast was clear for them. He was sought for days by the police, who finally caught up with him and took him to the detention center. Because he was a known addict, he was kept here for over a year while awaiting trial. This period was a low point for him because he finally realized what a null he was. He had the bad image of a "loser," whom everyone looked down upon. The "whole system" was against him; and he was no longer sure he could buck it, as in the past, and come out on top. He had a felony charge against him and was sure that, one way or another, they would try to trick him into pleading guilty and going to jail. Even the sympathetic people who wanted to help him, such as the correction officers and attendants, could not help him against the superior figure of the judge. Everyone was trying to break him down, and even those who were trying to help him felt that they could not because he had become so "implicated in the system."

When the judges tried to browbeat him into pleading guilty, however, he "felt the strength coming back" and again thought that he could fight the system. For some reason, he would not plead guilty and saw himself as a David against Goliath. He, a mere nobody, would buck the whole world and come out on top, even over the judges. One judge after another tried to break him down but didn't succeed since he refused to plead guilty. He felt he had done enough time already and was only willing to be placed on probation. He would rot in jail before he pleaded guilty. An interesting thing happened at this time in that the finger of his right hand needed to be taken off because it had become infected. This may have had some castration significance which absolved him from his guilt and his need to fight. As he put it, "Drugs left my mind when I realized the pain from the operation." With this, he felt he finally lost his desire to use heroin and wouldn't need to use it again. Primarily responsible for this feeling was his mother's standing by him, as well as the realization that he was dealing with society and couldn't possibly win. He nevertheless continued his efforts to intimidate the judges and outwit them. As he said, "They realized that I meant business." He stood up to them and they finally settled for getting him on probation. He pleaded guilty and got home in this way.

When he came to the mother's home he found everything closed, and he was frightened that she had died. He learned that she had been ill and was staying with his sister. He went to the sister's house expecting to be evicted, but was "flabbergasted" when they greeted him kindly and took him in again. He knew he would never use drugs again since he had had all he could take and was finally reassured by the fact of the mother's and sister's acceptance. He knew by now that he couldn't die. In the past, he had despised waking up in the cellar and seeing the dawn coming. He prayed to God that he would never wake up and hated the fact that he was still alive and didn't have the courage to kill himself. He had had a number of O.D.'s and reluctantly woke up from them knowing that he couldn't die and didn't have the will to do something about it. After the court episode, he decided he had to take responsibility for himself since he had to live and change. He asked his mother to help him. When he came home, everything was so clean and beautiful, and this too helped him realize a change was taking place. He had problems since he had no friends, but his sister began introducing him to her friends and taking him to meetings so that he was able to meet square people. He felt deeply that he had finally been vindicated: his mother had always said that she saw something good in him; and he now wanted to prove that the good part was the real him. He began trying to exorcise his devil and let something good in.

The first time he went to apply for a job he was worried that they would see the track marks on his arms, but surprisingly the doctor put the tourniquet on his arm and covered up the tracks, and he was able to get the job. He had been ready to run away to avoid confronting the doctor, but the "devil suddenly left" him, and he felt a beautiful spirit come in on his right side and strengthen him in his determination to see it through and not run away. He had paid and this was a sign that everything was working right for him now. God or some external being or spirit was now with him. He had had the same feeling in the courtroom when he was confronting the judges. He began moving into a better groove, got a job, and even became a union delegate. He married, but things didn't go well, and he was separated. His mother passed away in 1967. He changed increasingly after his marriage, pulling away from all former associations with drugs, although he found it hard at the beginning and still hung out at bars and in old drug-addict haunts. He was in the middle because he no longer had square friends, and his sister helped him bridge the gap to some extent. He had to continue making choices which would be constructive. But he found gradually that his whole life was changing. Again he seemed to be leading a double life because the new people he associated with would have been shocked if they knew about his previous life. He was now responsible and working and joined a number of organizations. He felt he was in a unique position to function because he could still "think with the criminal mind" which remained with him, but could also ignore it and function better in his new social setting.

He summarized this by saying that he had been through everything and had rebelled against everything. The thing that helped him make it was that there was nothing left to rebel against except being a drug addict, and he finally was able to do this too. He described himself as a born rebel, who was finally reduced to a nothing. When he realized he was a nothing and could not buck the system, he began to change. He has been trying to get his head screwed back on again ever since. Although he was able to make it without a program, his general advice would be that it was too rough to do it this way.

The interview ended here, but in a subsequent meeting, Mr. S. was able to conclude and explain his relationship with the therapeutic community where he stayed nine months. Apparently, he still felt a need to legitimize himself, and one of his thoughts— although he worked in private industry—was to become involved with a narcotics rehabilitation program. There were several reasons for this: he had "made" it himself and knew first-hand how to treat addicts; and he had also helped in the rehabilitation of his own sister. He was proud that he had been accorded the respect of having a probation officer in Philadelphia entrust her care to him, a former junkie. He liked the idea of working with addicts, which gave him recognition, and he was also tired of worrying that his addiction would be discovered and lead to his losing his job. He was persuaded to enter a residential center to get training in "encounters." He still did not have enough awareness of himself and was worried because he had been in so much trouble and needed to think seriously to make sure he was doing things right this time.

Here too, Mr. S. needed to underline his cleverness since he advanced rapidly to leadership in the therapeutic community. He liked the concern shown by the therapeutic community people, since residents would stay up all night to help people in trouble. He finally rebelled against the community, however, because he felt it had become a way of keeping him dependent. He was also angry that they had blocked his efforts at finding employment in another rehabilitation program. He left because he thought they were simply holding him down and he was beginning to regress.

CASE OF MR. S.   NO PROGRAM

Brotman-Freedman Typology
1. Normal conventionality   —
2. Criminality and hustling   —
3. Family conventionality   ?
4. Friends' conventionality   —
Classification: "Hustler"

Chein's Typology
Rebelling against stern father and society, envy of brothers, need to test mother's love.

Life Cycle
Confirmed street addict—in fact, sank so low that other street addicts scorned him because he lived in a coal pile in the cellar amid a terrible stench.

Social Milieu
Lexington—abroad in service, Philadelphia to New York.

Cloward-Ohlin
No clear "blocked opportunity." Not a "double loser" since he prided himself on ability to get ahead through illegitimate means. Not "retreatist" in sense of giving up desire for success, money, and status.

Case of Mrs. A.

This is a study of a thirty-five-year-old black girl of lower middle-class background with a brother who was also a narcotic addict.

Both claimed they had "made it" on their own, in terms of growing out of the addiction system without participation in any formal program, but it was clear that Mrs. A. had not yet worked out her many problems. She was not happy in her present isolated life and at times still needed to fall back on supports such as alcohol and, infrequently, other drugs. Through much of the interview, I found it difficult to define Mrs. A's manner, which was hearty, bluff, challenging, and provocative, until I realized she was instinctively treating me as a "John" in the manner she had undoubtedly used as a prostitute.

Tolerance for Addiction

FAMILY AND SOCIAL BACKGROUND. When asked directly about the role of her family in her addiction, Mrs. A. balked and denied that they had had anything to do with it: "They were marvelous! There were twelve of us, and I was the youngest." As she relaxed during the interview, the role of the family became rather clear. She felt that everyone older than she, both siblings and parents, "domineered" over her. Not only did they watch her and scrutinize all her ways, but they encouraged their friends in Philadelphia to keep an eye on her. There was therefore the early challenge of evading detection and doing what she wanted in defiance of the authority above her. She showed considerable ambivalence, saying on the one hand, "I was not a nice kid and hung out with a gang of ten girls who all went together"; yet, adding, she saw nothing wrong in her activities; it was "fun." Apparently, there was wonder and fascination in stealing, which was useful for kicks, but also practical in terms of getting clothing. She was tired of wearing the hand-me-downs of older siblings, and there was gratification in getting the clothing on her own. Clothing was important to her, and she saw nothing wrong in stealing it. There were numerous indications of such naive narcissism as well as psychopathy.

Mrs. A. was confused in relation to time and specific events and found it hard to pinpoint the years when she was going around with her gang, though it appeared to be in the latency years. She later seemed to believe that drugs had damaged or, at least, numbed her brain so that she now forgot easily. She characterized herself as "never a good girl." The recurring motif was the need for "fun," the desire to dress well, to go places and do things, and to be where the action was. Very early, she needed to choose between the world of the goody-goody and the bad girl, and she unhesitatingly chose the latter. Like her brother, she emphasized that her family was very strict, and there was no fun inside the house, so that she needed to look outside for kicks. Her mother worked "too hard," with twelve children; and the father drank, so she was raised by the older brothers and sisters. Not only did she and the gang steal from stores, but they also sneaked into movies and concerts for their fun. She generalized: "This was my childhood—stealing and having a good time with the girls."

She added that there were boys too, but no sexual experience, and she was a virgin until she was married. She was a tomboy who enjoyed playing basketball and other sports; and in this, seemed to be emulating her older brothers since she frequently went to watch them play. Although she went out with boys, it was as their equal and not to enjoy kissing or hugging. Later on, there was more than a hint of lesbian tendencies: her closest friend was a "bulldigger" or dyke, and she lived with her for a long time. In fact, she later also became involved in a "threesome," in which a man lived with two girls.

She was fondest of her older brother, who apparently stood *in loco parentis.* He was lovable and accepted her without condemnation no matter what she did. The father was an alcoholic, but she loved him "because he was my father. Why should I dislike him? He never harmed me." She said, "I did not like the good way because there was no fun in being good, and I did not know any goody-goody kids anyhow. My mother suggested I go out with the goody-goodies, but I found out that they were not so good." About her mother she said, "I loved her, loved her, loved her, and still do." As to the brother who said he had helped her make it off drugs, she claimed she had mixed feelings about him. She was fond of him, but he became a "bitch" when she grew stronger. She resented his influence and control over her and fought it. What she made clear was that her brother's wife had suspected "something funny going on between them," namely an incestuous relationship, and this was one of the reasons for the wife's leaving him.

As indicated, Mrs. A. saw nothing wrong in stealing or doing the things she did and still showed some confusion as to whether it had been wrong. She admitted that, "to some extent," she sometimes saw it as wrong when she looked back, but at that time she certainly could not see it. Her stealing did not hurt anyone; she liked her friends; she was having fun; and she had no problems. She stole clothes because she wanted to be dressed up, and clothes were important in her life. What was also important was that the ten girls dress exactly alike, and they therefore made sure to steal identical items so that they could wear the same shoes, sneakers, etc., and identify with each other. In terms of where she stood in the group, she said, "I was neither a leader nor a follower, but I was always there." She added that she would never be just a follower, but an in-betweener, and would never be left behind by anybody.

Regarding her school, she enjoyed going because all her friends were there, but she was never a good student. She was rather irritated when I mentioned that her brother had valued intellectuality and good marks in school, and she asked sharply that she not be compared with him and that I speak only of her. She was a marginal student and barely graduated from high school. Because of her conduct, she was not permitted to be on stage at graduation and remained in the audience. She did not like the idea of being square and wearing a white dress and shoes, and this was another reason why she did not care to be on stage. She never really learned anything in school, but simply went. In fact, she never really learned anything until recently.

Her youthful ambition was to be a telephone operator, and also a model. She is sorry she never managed the latter, but she was a telephone operator in Philadelphia and later in New York. She was the first black telephone operator in Philadelphia and was greatly cherished as a telephone operator in New York because of her "fancy" Philadelphia accent.

Interestingly, Mrs. A. appeared to think of her childhood life as square; she moved more forcibly from the square world only about the time she was graduating from high school. She began to get into the other life and mixed with people from the other side of the tracks, people who were involved with heroin and reefers. To these people, she appeared as a square and a good girl since she did not hang around corners, but was actually working with the telephone company. She admitted she had been arrested because of her youthful stealing episodes and was held at the precinct several times. On these occasions, her parents and siblings made no move to come and bail her out. It was usually the mother of a girl friend who did this for her.

EXPERIMENTATION. She began working in a Philadelphia department store in her last year of high school. She was selling sweaters in the men's department and met very sharp men from the other side of the tracks who wore fancy cashmere coats and kangaroo shoes. Since she was selling cashmere sweaters, they gravitated to her and said sweet things to her. She was fascinated by them and readily made a date when invited. They were smoking reefers at that time, and she did not hesitate when they suggested she join them. She went full speed ahead, and liked the marijuana because it made her feel so good. She was able to eat better and felt happier. She also liked one of the fellows and began going out with him at the age of sixteen. She emphasized that there was no sex, "It never entered my mind." To them also, she was a good girl from the other side of the tracks, and she was still in school. Through them, she learned to go for way-out music like jazz and for pot at the same time. After a while, she began going out with the friend of this first man and eventually married him.

She was graduated from high school in 1953 and did not begin heroin until 1957. She first claimed never to have used pills, but then admitted she had mixed pills extensively with heroin during the period when she was out of control and was no longer concerned about the effect they might have on her. The men were already using heroin, but she did not know it at the time. Her husband worked briefly as a chauffeur for show people and moved in fast circles. When her mother moved to New York in 1952, she had to make a choice; she decided to stay in Philadelphia. She was then working for the telephone company and waiting for a transfer. Her brother was still there. She did not know her brother was using drugs since they were rarely in each other's company although they had been close in the family, but they now moved in different circles.

Mrs. A. still seemed to be vacillating between being a good girl and a bad girl, since she simultaneously had the ambition to be somebody and to be thought well of by everybody. Still, she was fascinated with devious things and could not say no to anything. She was also crazy about her job and being the first long-distance operator. With all this, she was hanging out with people who were doing awful things, as she discovered later. Through her husband, she was attracted to the bright lights. He had a Cadillac, and his grandmother had a great deal of money. Only later did she learn that the grandmother ran houses which were used as brothels. During the interview, Mrs. A. repeatedly made slips which indicated that she thought of this woman not as her husband's grandmother, but as her own; and, in fact, as her own good mother, who stood by her and came to her rescue whenever she was in trouble.

The time finally came for her to move to New York when she got her transfer, and her husband later visited her every weekend. She hated Brooklyn and loved Philadelphia, and traveled back and forth. At that time, her husband was on heroin and was sick, and she helped him without being aware of what was involved. She lived in New York with a girl friend who was a model and a good girl. As a result, Mrs. A. did not do anything wrong.

When she returned to Philadelphia, it was arranged that she live in the building, which was a brothel, owned by the grandmother. Mrs. A. was fascinated by the prostitutes and saw nothing wrong with falling into it herself. This happened without any struggle or effort on her part, and she began prostituting by simply following her husband's crowd. All the girls she knew were prostituting, and she was proud of being the youngest and slickest chick in the whole group. The whole scene seemed beautiful to her, since the money came in so easily. It was summertime, and "the living was easy." Her boyfriend had been brought up in this world and, of course, he saw nothing wrong with it or with her joining in and giving him the money. He was a pimp, but "he belonged to me as my boyfriend alone." She was still not on heroin at this time.

Tolerance for Abstinence—Addiction

When her husband visited in New York, he left some white stuff behind for the times when he came in. She noticed it and was encouraged by some of his friends to try it. She began by snorting, and the first time threw up, got sick, and swore she would never use it again. When her boyfriend learned she was experimenting, he did not mind since, if she were hooked, she could hustle better, and it would be useful. She therefore began prostituting and using drugs at the same time, and one reinforced the other. The heroin stimulated her, and she could go out with more vigor to pick up Johns. It made the whole thing more tolerable, although she emphasized that she enjoyed the prostitution in and of itself as well; she met such interesting and important people.

In time, she needed the prostitution to support her habit and also to hold onto her husband by giving him money. She did not stay long with snorting, but went on to mainlining and, in fact, got hooked very fast. When she learned she was hooked, it did not bother her, since she simply felt she would have to earn more to get more drugs. She was not frightened as long as she had enough money for it. She began spending from one hundred dollars to one hundred forty dollars a day on drugs.

She was living with her husband although not yet married to him. The first time she was "busted" was in 1955 when she was sentenced for prostitution and disorderly conduct. She was also pregnant and was delivered of her first child in jail. She learned that her grandmother was a very powerful person, since she intervened to have her transferred to a better prison.

Regarding her pregnancy, she said that she had wanted and accepted it. Since she could not take care of the baby and do the things she did, she gave the baby over to her grandmother. She increasingly began to hate her husband since he never did anything for her, but simply used her. But the grandmother came through with the bail, the bondsman, and the lawyer, and was concerned about her, even blaming her grandson for the things he was doing to her.

She was now beginning to be caught in a treadmill, since she had to start prostituting all over again and using drugs. In reflecting now why she went back to this life, she said that she was still young and healthy and saw nothing wrong with prostituting or even with drug use. It seemed a "natural step" to her. She had "good feelings" about what she was doing and took pride in the fact that she could earn between $100 and $150 on a Sunday afternoon. She was puzzled that she should have grown into this life "so fast and furious." While she enjoyed the life of prostitution at the beginning because it was so free and easy, other problems nevertheless developed very soon: increasing scrutiny by the police and arrests made her life hazardous and uncomfortable. She expressed increasing hostility toward her husband, saying that he had not earned a dime in his entire life. This got on her nerves as she realized he was only using her and her money for drugs. "He just sat by and shot dope all the time."

She was again arrested and served a year in jail, then returned to her grandmother. Her husband began staying out nights, and she learned he was going out with other girls. She left him and marveled that, although she had done everything he wanted, he was still not satisfied and had to look for other girls. She went to live with his friend, but this was a repetition of life with her husband since this man was also a user and pimp, and exploited her similarly for dope. Her life with him was "no better and no worse" than with her husband. In time, it became very uncomfortable, and "it began to feel like hell all the way around." The money was beautiful, but it was not being used in any meaningful way. After a while, the man got busted and needed to leave Philadelphia. She learned that he was married already. This was the only time she grew afraid since she was becoming increasingly uncomfortable with the Philadelphia scene and had to come to New York. In Philadelphia she knew the police and the Johns, but she knew nothing about New York, and it took her a long time to learn what it was about. She had heard that the police paraded around like Johns, and she lived in fear that she would be arrested any moment.

Tolerance for Abstinence

Her life was therefore becoming increasingly uncomfortable and full of strains. Friends began ratting on her, and she was uncomfortable now in both Philadelphia and New York. She was beginning to feel as if she were sinking down to the gutter and beginning to reach rock bottom. She had to do more desperate things to get her drugs since she could not earn enough prostituting because she was watched so closely. She began to write prescriptions for Dolophines and other drugs. She was caught one time in a drugstore and was again arrested by the police because she had stolen the prescriptions from a hospital and forged them. She was handled roughly, but managed to escape by jumping out of the police car. The police now began searching for her and she could no longer comfortably earn money as a prostitute. She learned that there was a time between the day and evening shifts when the police changed their shift, and she sneaked out then to pick up Johns and hurriedly earn what she could to support her habit.

She was living with a girl friend who was a lesbian and with a man, a square, who was a construction worker; all three shared the house. She was rather proud that she was still the money-maker of the household. By this time, she had two babies and did not know who the father of the second baby was. Her two baby girls were "black and white and beautiful." There was a crisis when her grandmother was taken sick and could not take care of the babies. It was necessary for her to go there to take care of the grandmother and the children. The man who was sharing the apartment did not relish the idea of her leaving and informed against her. The police arrested her, and she was jailed in a terrible place. Again, the grandmother intervened and got her out for Christmas in time to be with the children, for which she was very grateful. Later she did more time and was then placed on parole. After this she returned home, but "went back to the same old shit."

She emphasized that she only had two boyfriends in her life, neither of them any good. They exploited her to the hilt and soured her on subsequent relationships. She tried to stay away from drugs, but gravitated back inevitably.

At this time, past events began to telescope and she could no longer remember things clearly except that they were all awful and repetitious. She was so confused now about her inability to remember that she thought her brain had been damaged by drugs. She began to associate with a dealer and acted as his lookout, since he was being sought by the police. The police were aware of this and began to resent her because she was helping the man evade detection. She also helped others evade arrest by pointing out the police to prostitutes and Johns. The police felt she was too hip and they therefore barred her from the streets so that she could only go out in the dark. In this, she seemed to resemble her brother, who described with pride his exploits in evading authority and in being able to manipulate and outwit adults and society toward her own ends. She suddenly took pride in her abilities and associations in higher circles, since her involvement with white dealers, big-time whores, and pimps made her something of a big shot herself. The police would have liked her to set the dealer up for arrest, but she refused to cooperate with them. She strung the police along, but they finally caught up with her and she was sent away for fifteen months for prostitution.

She was released to do day work in a doctor's office as part of a rehabilitation program they had instituted. There was cough syrup all over the doctor's office, and she had quite a picnic drinking up for more than four months.

REHABILITATION. By this time, Mrs. A. felt she had really reached rock bottom. Although she had neglected to mention it earlier, she had five babies by now, none of whom she could take responsibility for. She had a special attachment for the first child, a daughter by the husband. The other children were being taken care of by a brother who was very strict with them and reluctant to release them to her care. She was terribly tired, guilty, and anxious to get back to her children whom she had neglected so badly. She compared herself with her mother and felt she was not doing as adequate a job as her mother had with her twelve children. This was reinforced by her mother's death. She exclaimed, "Wow!" and only now fully sensed that drugs had gotten her into a great deal of trouble. She realized that she was not doing what she was supposed to be doing with her life. She was again pregnant and again in jail when she learned of her mother's death. She had begun mixing heroin with pills and was sure it had affected her mind. She mentioned there had actually been a sixth child that she was reluctant to talk about since it was born mentally retarded. She thought the pills had affected her brain as well as the child's, and this was the reason for the child's mental retardation.

She had been in jail a year and a half now, was going out of her mind, and felt ready to flip. She was out of her senses and talked obsessively about her childhen and her neglect of them. She began weighing what she could do with the rest of her life and thought that, while she might continue being a prostitute, she simply had to give up drugs which were destroying her. She rationalized that prostitution was not habit-forming and would not ruin her health or hurt her in any way, but there was everything wrong with being a drug addict. You had to steal, rob, lie, and not be a human being, and she was tired of it. The turning point finally came in the police precinct as she was being fingerprinted before being jailed. She decided that she must stop using drugs because it was a losing game. She vowed to herself that, by thirty, she would no longer be a prostitute or on drugs, since one seemed to lead to the other. She thought that being thirty was being an old lady, and she had no business selling her body at this time although there had been nothing wrong with it at eighteen. She was like a little jitterbug at that age, young and anxious to experience everything without any delayed gratification. She had no concern about morals, lived for the moment, but now worried terribly about her children.

Her children were a major factor in helping her decide she must stop. They had been writing her indicating that they needed her help, and she felt she must respond. By this time, she had been on drugs and also prostituting for ten years. She was utterly weary of jails and the street scene, the fact that people were watching her, and that she had to lie, con, and hustle continuously. It was time for her to stop; she was getting old. "My body and my mind were tired. I reached rock bottom; I weighed ninety pounds, and I was ready to flip out of my mind at the point when I went into jail the last time."

In discussing the role her brother had played in her rehabilitation, she thought that she had already achieved most of the change by herself, but admitted that her brother's ability to get her out of jail on parole ("since nobody else would have me") was also important in helping her make it. She expressed some anger toward him because he would not let her do anything or go anywhere and was "worse than the worst probation officer at first." Still, maybe this was what she needed then. She thought she had outgrown him by now, and there were many elements in which she was now stronger than he and could now help him with. She added that "Somehow I have gotten very strong now, and I feel much older and wiser and not crazy. I never think about drugs unless my brother happens to mention it." She did not know how she got so strong, since she had nobody to help her, but believes it was her children who did it. For three years she had to wait to get them back. She emphasized, "I am their mother and they loved me. They could not understand why I was not with them, and this weighed on me."

In discussing her present life, Mrs. A. at first said, "My life is beautiful now since I stay home and devote twenty-four hours to the care of my babies and never go anywhere. After not having them for so long, there is joy in being with them, taking care of them, and seeing them grow." There had been no happiness in drugs. On the other hand, she admitted to some negative feelings about her present life, saying that she did not know anybody and was quite lonely. In looking back, she felt she had been brutally used by the two men in her life, and she was now so conditioned and attuned to exploitation that she could not tolerate any man and expected the worst. Yet she misses men, since she always enjoyed their companionship and enjoyed sex. She emphasized that "sex is never sickening if you enjoy it." She concluded that, while she knows she has done "marvelously," at the same time she feels her life is empty since she does not go anywhere and is living too sheltered a life. She is still young, loves to dance, and to see young people enjoy themselves, and would like to be part of this. There is no generation gap as far as she is concerned since she still considers herself a "swinger." She had not resolved her feelings about prostitution and said she might go back to it, especially if she had no money for her babies. However, she would not look for it if she could manage any other way, including stealing. In other ways she showed her continuing ambivalence and admitted that she has emotional problems. She stated that she would like a psychiatrist to find out why she is afraid to get out of the house.

Since Mrs. A. wanted to avoid people, she preferred being alone even while working and chose the night shift from twelve to eight. She filled in the nights by drinking and was on the verge of becoming an alcoholic. Fortunately, she pulled out of it and has not been drinking now for some time. She would never go back to drugs because of the life it involved.

In talking about her daughter, Mrs. A. revealed her own dependency and need to lean on her children at times as if they were parents and companions.

There was evidence of strong masochistic tendencies in that she was ready to submerge herself with men and let herself be used as a prostitute to support two pimps in their drug habits. It is possible she had some identification with her father in her drug addiction and alcoholism.

In thinking about the elements which helped her grow out of her addiction, it is clear as in our other studies that the life of prostitution, and the drug use which went with it, became increasingly intolerable and maladjustive. She gradually exhausted all resources, lost track of time, went out of control, and mixed heroin with pills to knock herself out, even though she felt pills would injure her brain and affect her children. The life of prostitution and drugs in Philadelphia, as well as New York, became more and more intolerable since she was constantly being scrutinized by the police and could no longer go out on the street to hustle. The joys of prostitution were outweighed by the hazards and penalties. Toward the end, she felt she was losing her mind. She was also burdened with guilt about her neglect of the children, especially in comparison with the image of the mother who was able to care for her twelve children. There was tremendous guilt about the child who was mentally retarded since she felt that her use of pills was responsible for this.

One of the important motivations in her making it, therefore, was the fact that she needed to take care of her children and could do so only by getting off drugs. She also felt she was getting too old to be acting like a jitterbugger, and she made a resolution that she must be off by the age of thirty. Although in the interview with her brother, he claimed to be primarily responsible for helping her change, she made it clear that she had already determined to change her way of life herself, and the brother was simply a helping person who contributed to it.

She was aware that her problems had not ended with her getting off heroin use. She was aware that she still had numerous problems to be worked out and asked about a psychiatrist, which was, in fact, a challenge to me to learn whether I could not assume a helping role with her. Actually, she had achieved abstinence at a cost of deprivation in other areas of her life, though she is achieving much gratification by taking care of her children. He life is nevertheless empty, and she misses essential human relationships, sex, and meaningful work. She is now in a counterphobic retreat from the world that is helping her achieve stability, but which might yet go by the board in a crisis.

CASE OF MRS. A.   MADE IT ON OWN–NO PROGRAM
Brotman-Freedman Typology
    1. Normal conventionality   −
    2. Criminality and hustling   −
    3. Family conventionality   +
    4. Friend conventionality   −
    Classification: "Hustler" (?)

Chein's Typology

Competition with mother and rebellion against father. Desire for clothes and nice things—saw no harm in stealing and prostitution or using drugs.

Life Cycle

Went through all phases and became confirmed street addict.

Social Milieu

Philadelphia to New York—after Lexington did not return to old neighborhood but took up with drug users.

Cloward-Ohlin

No real "blocked opportunity"—had chances to succeed. Surrendered conventional goals to prostitute and use drugs, but never lost sight of these goals.

VI

FINDINGS

DESPITE THE VARIED cases used in this study, it seems possible to generalize a number of specific findings which will be elaborated in this concluding section.

THE CHRONOLOGY OF ADDICTION AND DE-ADDICTION

An examination of the ages at which the ex-addicts started and stopped using heroin is interesting:[6]

1. As anticipated, the ex-addicts studied began using heroin while still fairly young. The median age of initiation to heroin was seventeen years and the range was from thirteen to seventeen years.

2. The respondents used heroin for a long time—a median period of nine years. The actual range was from a minimum of four years to a maximum of twenty-one years.

3. The median age at which the subjects stopped using heroin was twenty-six years, or slightly less than the thirty and over years suggested in Winick's maturing out theory.[16]

4. Interestingly, those who began using heroin when they were younger used it for a shorter period than those who started when they were older. Of those who began between the ages of thirteen and seventeen, the mean length of addiction was eight years; for those who started between the ages of eighteen and twenty-seven, the mean length of addiction was fifteen and a half years.

These findings, if they can be generalized to the entire population of ex-addicts, offer a dilemma for those attempting to plan treatment. If addiction can be expected to run for a certain number of years, the strongest efforts at rehabilitation should be concentrated on those who have used heroin longest. However, those who have used heroin longest would also be the oldest.

111

Interestingly, those who start young appear on the basis of our preliminary figures to use heroin for a shorter time than those who start older. The meaning of this is not readily apparent unless it relates to the greater availability of effective treatment resources. It is possible that, in methadone programs, the addicts who made it are a select population for whom the addictive life became increasingly maladaptive and who were therefore prepared to give up their addiction and assume conventional roles.[6]

THE FIRST SERIOUS EFFORT TO ABSTAIN

The twenty-three respondents interviewed by survey methods made a serious voluntary effort to stop using heroin considerably before they kicked the habit the last time. Sixteen of these underwent voluntary detoxification with the idea of abstention; two switched their milieux in an effort to give up heroin; four abstained voluntarily following some trauma; and one got married in order to overcome his addiction.

For the fifteen people for whom we have information, the first serious voluntary effort at detoxification occurred a long time before the final abstention. The median age for this period was twenty-two, or eight years before the median age of complete cessation of heroin use. Most of those who stopped made a serious effort to do so several years before they were finally successful.

Although many addicts began to use drugs gradually and took a year or longer to develop a daily habit, often they did not stop using in the same gradual fashion. Many of the respondents were heavy users up to the time of their final abstention; their heroin use did not dwindle off and finally fade away. In others, the transition was more gradual. This suggests, also, that many addicts who believe they can resume using heroin occasionally without become re-addicted are fooling themselves.[6]

ACCOUNTING SCHEME FOR THE PROCESS OF DE-ADDICTION

Examination of the thirty-one cases reveals that rarely or never was there one single reason for a person's giving up addiction. Behavioral scientists who have studied the decision-making process have developed accounting schemes to deal with all the elements affecting a given decision: an accounting scheme to describe why a person bought a particular brand of toothpaste assumes that the quality of the product is not the main consideration. The reasons, rather, would be broken down into the "pushes and pulls." [In addiction, there is the time element. Many decisions are made over a substantial period of time.)

An accounting scheme for the de-addiction process must therefore comprise what we have termed a series of "pushes" and "pulls." The pushes include those features of addictive life which are stressful, maladaptive, and increasingly intolerable. The pulls relate to those factors which help draw the addict towards changing his way of life, such as the hold of former "square" values and the possibility of finding a way out of his addiction. To recap, the push is the situation in which the addict finds himself as he feels his addictive life increasingly intolerable and nonfunctional. Often he seems to be falling into a final, destructive slide, which we have characterized as "rock bottom." The pull is the attraction of the treatment facility and former square values which were never really relinquished. The treatment program must offer the addict initial hope, even though he may not seriously intend to benefit from it at the time he enters the program. In some cases, as in that of I.R., the subject has no belief that the facility can help him, but enters it because he has no other place to go.[6]

The life cycle model described, comprises the various stages through which an addict, specifically "the street addict," passes rather than a generalized model for all addicts and ex-addicts. There are two major phases: transition to addiction and transition to abstinence. The major aspect of this process is that it evolves slowly with a great deal of learning and adaptation required in each phase and numerous decisions to be made along the way. The neophyte changes psychologically and physiologically as he becomes a street addict and gradually learns to survive in the new tribal subculture of addiction. To become a square again and learn how to readjust to living in a world without drugs similarly requires much learning in addition to a tolerance for abstinence. The fact that the ex-addicts studied used heroin for a median period of nine years demonstrates that, for most heroin users, the life cycle of addiction is a long, painstaking, and ultimately frantic process.

In reviewing our thirty-one cases, it is clear that just as there were many complicated factors, processes, and decisions associated with "selecting" heroin addiction as a career choice, so were there numerous elements associated with the de-addiction process. This is substantiated by the fact that a considerable period of time elapsed between the first serious voluntary efforts to stop using drugs and the complete cessation of drug use.

Before starting the study, the author felt that four basic elements needed to be considered in examining the de-addiction process. First was the real situation in which the heroin addict finds himself: in the United States, he is most likely to be in trouble with the police and to have difficulty maintaining an increasingly expensive illegal habit. This was conceptualized as a *push* to get him out of the addiction system. There are also a number of *pulls*. First among these are the drug user's relatives and friends who attempt to persuade him to stop using drugs and help him become an ex-addict. Second are the increasing numbers of effective treatment facilities now existent. The third pull is the value system of the majority culture in the United States, with its emphasis on respectability, material rewards, and the work ethic. A fourth factor undoubtedly important in the de-addiction process is the ego strength of the addict and the personal resources at his command. The person who is better adjusted and educated, more intelligent, with developed job skills and less total involvement in the addiction system would be more likely to return readily to the non-addicted society. It is a combination of these pushes and pulls and the increasing maladaptiveness of the addictive life which account for successful de-addiction. We shall attempt to describe some of these pushes and pulls in greater detail in the succeeding section.[6]

THE PUSHES OF ADDICTION—MALADAPTIVENESS OF THE ADDICTIVE LIFE OF THE HEROIN ADDICT

At the start of heroin addiction, drug use serves many purposes. Chein postulated that there are two principal reasons for using drugs. As indicated earlier, heroin has certain positive psychopharmacological effects: it reduces tension and creates a "high." This can be pleasurable and can also help the drug user escape his personal problems. It permits him to screen out unpleasant reality or cop out of facing the problems of adulthood. The second major function served by drug use is social. The heroin user becomes a part of a social group. He establishes an identity in a separate culture with its own language and mores. He belongs. This may be an effective way of rebelling against society and feeling less alienated.[1]

At the beginning, the heroin user is likely to be aware principally of the positive aspects of drug use. He is in the "honeymoon" phase. If he is selling drugs, he may have found a source of ready money which is a means to upward mobility and glamour when legitimate means are denied him. There are the pleasant physical effects and the pleasure of new experiences and "kicks." For many, there may be a prolonged period when the living is easy as Mrs. B. described it.

As the heroin user is pulled deeper into the addiction system and needs more and more heroin to maintain his habit, he must begin to steal or engage in prostitution for money. The problems increase, and the initial glamour fades. He is likely to be arrested repeatedly and become known to the police as a thief and heroin addict. He will lose his job if he has one and experience rejection by his family and square friends. Life becomes a rat race as he engages in a day-in, day-out struggle to support his habit and maintain his connections. Heroin use then becomes extremely dysfunctional for most addicts and is increasingly perceived as such by them even though they continue to love the "beautiful feeling" of heroin use. Institutionalized heroin users who have used drugs for a long time are very likely to view with disdain the life of the addict and to have a very negative picture of themselves while they are using. This self-hatred may be reflected in their frequent designation of themselves as "dope fiends."

The principal impetus for giving up addiction thus derives from the fact that long-term heroin use in time becomes highly maladaptive in our society, and addicts become tired of their grinding existence. This can be attributed, at least in part, to the difficulty of obtaining heroin and supporting a habit. Obviously, if high-quality, inexpensive heroin were readily accessible, and our society adopted a less punitive stance, this situation would not prevail.

The twenty-one survey respondents when asked, "Objectively, why did you stop using drugs?" gave as their principal response the fact that they had grown tired of the life.

Juan, a Puerto Rican male in his late twenties, said:

"I got tired of the abuse I was undergoing. In jail they take away your identity—you just exist there. First I got tired of other people treating me badly, then I got tired of the way I was treating myself. I realized I was destroying myself. I was tired of that kind of life also; the whole scene was a drag after a while."

Rafael, a Puerto Rican male in his mid-twenties, said:

"I looked at myself, I saw that I had lost everything: school, jobs. I lost my image of myself and my dignity. I was an animal. I was physically run down. I felt that I had to do something with my life."

Pedro, a Puerto Rican male in his mid-twenties, said:

"I was aware that I was destroying myself. I was always sick. Physically I was weak. I was unhappy. I didn't belong in the dope world."

Though the case history respondents also confirmed that they had grown tired of the drug life, one further dimension emerged. Many of them actually felt that they had hit an especially low point in their lives. This low point, which we termed "rock bottom" was a very important push which impelled many of our respondents to seek help:

Mr. S., a black man in his late thirties, is now extremely fastidious, and says that he was this way before he started using heroin. As we saw, rock bottom for him came when his life of heroin addiction made it impossible for him to keep clean. He slept in rat-infested cellars that frequently drained human refuse when the toilets overflowed. He developed pustular fungus sores all over his body. He stopped minding the smells which repelled other people. He felt that he became an outcast even among other junkies who could not understand how he lived that way. He slept on piles of coal in the cellar, using his money for heroin rather than rent.

We noted, similiarly, that his sister at first found it relatively easy to pay for her heroin through prostitution. Eventually, she became known to the police as an addict and could no longer easily earn her money as a prostitute. She had to sneak out onto the street when the police were changing shifts, as otherwise she felt she would be spotted and arrested. Not only could she no longer earn money as a prostitute, but she was unable to support the six children that she had borne; one of whose mental retardation she blamed on her own drug use. She was down to 90 pounds and felt that her mind was going. She came to feel that drugs were destroying her. She wondered how a human being could use $150 worth of drugs a day. Furthermore, she felt that although it might be all right for a girl of eighteen to be a prostitute, it was unacceptable for a thirty-year-old.

Rock bottom need not necessarily be an objective or realistic low point; it may at times be highly subjective. Although the nature of rock bottom varied greatly among our respondents, many, in fact, did suffer extreme pain and deprivation. Just as many heroin users felt that certain turning points led them to become addicts, so many believed there were changes or crises which helped them out of their addiction. Often, this was the awareness of having hit their own particular nadir, or inability to survive a specific crisis or series of crises. Some of the situations in which our respondents found themselves were so acute and their resources so depleted that it is remarkable they could mobilize themselves to alter their lives.

The question naturally arises, "Why, if heroin use becomes so dysfunctional, do not all heroin addicts eventually become ex-addicts?" The answer may be that although drug users do become discouraged with the system or important elements of the system, a number of powerful reinforcements and adaptive values conspire to keep them encapsulated and pull them back repeatedly after release from treatment facilities or correctional institutions. In many cases, it is the problems which first impelled them to use heroin plus the later conditioning and reinforcing factors which are responsible for their repeated relapses. It is also difficult to abstain from drugs when one lives in a high-drug-use area and is surrounded by drug users who are long-standing cronies and friends.

The fact that the addict is known to the authorities as a drug user and has the stigma of a junkie and criminal also impedes rehabilitation. It is difficult for him to get a driver's license, be bonded, rent an apartment, secure employment, and make new friends. All these factors combine to make abstention difficult even when he is desperately seeking a way out. He has lost most or all of his contacts in the square world and finds it most difficult to work his way back to conventional living.[6]

Although treatment facilities played a major role in overcoming addiction, institutionalization does not in itself insure rehabilitaton. Many addicts adopt a life style whereby they spend most of their lives in jails or institutions and only occasionally venture out into the real world to use drugs, secure in the knowledge they will soon be safe behind bars again. A number of institutionalized users who had spent large portions of their adult life in jail reported they had grown quite accustomed to, and comfortable with being in jail and learned the best routines for "doing time" properly. The facilities were clean, the regimen predictable, and there were three meals a day. In many ways, it was an improvement over the harried street life of the addict. Institutionalization may nevertheless offer addicts who are constantly on the run and never face themselves a controlled setting where they can pause to look at themselves and their problems. The question arises, "Why did friends and relatives play such a minor role in the process of de-addiction?" The answer may well reside in the nature of the relationships established by addicts prior to and during their addiction. In many cases, relations with parents were at best poor and often destructive, contributing appreciably to the addiction itself. In brief, these addicts were not individuals who could establish intimate, long-term relationships with people in a position to help them become de-addicted.

A further factor is that the process of becoming a heroin addict is long and arduous. The period of addiction itself was also long for our sample of addicts. During this time, the addicts exhausted their "social credit" and relationships which could be productive. They borrowed or stole from their square friends, relatives, and associates. By the time they had hit rock bottom and were ready to stop using drugs, they were likely to have used up all possible sources of help.

THE "PULLS" OF TREATMENT PROGRAMS

In our sample, primarily obtained through treatment facilities, personal relationships within treatment facilities were important in the process of de-addiction. Each treatment facility seemed to appeal to certain types of drug users who accepted its ideology. Subsequent relationships with the program after the person had become an ex-addict were similarly important.

One of the problems in studying a particular treatment program is that persons with a long history of problems or trouble, such as the heroin addicts in our study, engaged in numerous attempts at rehabilitation over a long period of time. No one factor can be singled out as responsible for a person's having become de-addicted. Almost all survey respondents had been involved in at least one treatment program prior to the treatment program which finally worked. Earlier, "unsuccessful" treatment programs were often seen in retrospect as having been quite important, and having had a delayed impact.

> Juan, a Puerto Rican in his late twenties, left Riverside Hospital in 1960 but continued to use drugs for five more years. He stopped using drugs without enrolling in another program. This is how he remembers Riverside Hospital, at which he would be regarded as an unsuccessful case:
> "The person who helped me the most was my therapist at Riverside, who I saw in 1960. She socked reality to me when I was a kid. She was very helpful. She told me the truth, which I denied, but it stayed with me. Even though I rebelled against what she told me, later on when I was in prison, I thought about her a lot."

Another patient felt that a state institution from which he was discharged as "intractable" actually proved the turning point in his addiction career, though he was considered a failure at the time.

In discussing the treatment facilities which helped get them over their addiction, the ex-addicts spoke of the importance of their relationships with both staff and other participants in the program.

> Irving, a Jewish man in his late thirties, replied to the question about who had helped him by answering, "The whole Synanon house. I liked it when I could express anger and they weren't punitive, like the institutions I had been in."
>
> Rafael, a Puerto Rican in his middle twenties, reported of Damascus Church: "Everybody there gave me help. I needed to talk to someone, to find myself. They helped me toward this goal. They were sympathetic and understanding. They cried over me and even beat me, like real parents."

An important part of the treatment facility is its leaders and high-ranking staff, who may have charisma and become symbols of care and concern—"parent-figures." Those in the religious programs mentioned the personal importance of the churches' ministers to them. Likewise, several of those in the methadone maintenance program mentioned the charisma of Dr. Nyswander. The Synanon people were all personally touched by Chuck Diedrich. The care, concern, and personal interest evidenced by the relatively small number of leaders and directors of treatment programs are therefore seen as quite important. In many cases, the treatment program and its leadership substituted for the personal relationships which the addict was previously unable to achieve or which had been destroyed. Just as the addict had earlier belonged to something by being part of a group of drug users and losers, so did he now achieve a new sense of belonging through the treatment program.[6]

Some of the respondents spoke with bitterness about treatment facilities in which the staff demonstrated a lack of care or concern. It is possible to understand why the staff of some treatment facilities, especially detoxification centers, may appear to the addict as non-caring. It is well known in the field of public health that the recidivism rate for heroin addicts is very high. Frequently, workers entering the field have high hopes about the rehabilitation they will be able to bring about. However, when they see the same patients returning again and again and realize that their rescue fantasies about addicts have not been fulfilled, they become discouraged and may protect themselves by adopting bureaucratic procedures or by denying their concern. With such an attitude and approach, the centers will fail to reach the small number of addicts ready to give up drugs or fail to contribute something which could eventually become a factor in the de-addiction process—unless such repetitive detoxifications add to the eventual cumulative maladaptiveness of the addictive life.

Each of the programs has its own ideology which is generally accepted by those who are successful "graduates" of the program. Not only do the graduates of the various programs accept the ideology of their own program, but they are likely to reject the ideology of other programs. Those who have been successful in religious programs accept the idea that they were evil persons and sinners who were defying God. Now that they have given up drugs, they are following God's will and, in attempting to help others stop using drugs, are doing the work of God. The body is God's Temple and should not be defiled. Even smoking and drinking can defile the body. Those who have been cured by religious programs such as the Damascus Church and Teen Challenge feel that they were previously sinners and "bastards" and did not know the true path. Now they have found the proper faith and have the answer. They tend to deny the existence of prior psychological or physiological problems as responsible either for their addiction or their becoming drug-free. Ten of the eleven ex-addicts interviewed in the religious programs were either Puerto Rican or of Cuban and South American ethnic. The programs have much of the evangelistic, Pentecostal flavor of the Fundamentalist churches which are important in the Puerto Rican culture in the United States.

The Synanon belief is that the addict has personality problems, a "character disorder," and is "immature" and "irresponsible." Through attack therapy, an attempt is made to break down defenses and get the addict to face up to his inadequacies, following the AA model. Through the use of role models, he is shown appropriate, mature, square behavior. The Synanon ex-addicts interviewed accepted this ideology; they viewed their addiction as resulting from immaturity and felt that the program had indeed helped them grow up.

The methadone maintenance program also has its ideology. It is that the problem of addiction is based on neither weakness of character nor a search for Utopia, but rather a "metabolic deficiency." Once the addict has been stabilized on methadone, a narcotic blockade is established and the narcotic hunger satisfied. He then no longer craves heroin and can move to find employment and get his personal life in order. They view their problem as physical rather than psychological and believe that the important thing is to get a steady job and learn to lead a responsible life. Neither sin nor psychological factors are seen as important.

Graduates of the various programs accepted the ideology of their particular program and used it as an organizing force in their new life as ex-addicts. While a program's ideology may seem overly simplistic and unrealistic to the outside observer, it plays an important role for the person trying to overcome the problem. Not only does it provide guidelines on how to live in the future, but it helps explain his past irrational, antisocial behavior and, to this extent, tempers his personal guilt and simplifies the problem of rehabilitation.

Treatment facilities also have meaning in terms of the previous life of the addict and the finding of new incentives which can be picked up in terms of current needs. For example, the Synanon "games" seem to appeal especially to middle-class, white, often Jewish patients who can participate in these complicated intellectual and personalized encounters. Cyclazocine required strong motivation, high frustration tolerance, and good defenses, and was especially important, therefore, for middle-class people with strong motivation and roots in the community. It might also be useful for neophyte users if reinforced by probation or parole supervision.[19, 20] Methadone maintenance offered a powerful support for individuals who need to return to a ghetto environment such as Harlem and remain immune to the surrounding heroin activities. Ex-addict graduates of Daytop Village or Phoenix House or Synanon itself were, of course, reinforced by the factor of remaining within the orbit of their parent organization, which became the equivalent "shield" of a chemical approach such as cyclazocine or methadone maintenance.

It would be interesting to study the different approaches in terms of their effectiveness for different kinds of patients. This is being projected in the multimodality approach being conducted at the New York State Narcotic Addiction Control Commission. By building in evaluation and research, it is hoped to learn which approach works best for what kind of addicts and develop effective criteria for screening for treatment.[21]

THE PATH TOWARDS REHABILITATION: THE ROLE OF OTHER PEOPLE

Studies of occupational choice underline the importance of parents, relatives, teachers, and role models in the selection of occupations. Studies of older people have shown the enduringness of relationships and the importance of relationships with other people. Older women are sustained by contact with their children, grandchildren, and other relatives with whom they are engaged in meaningful activities.

We would have expected that other people, such as parents, spouses, and friends, would have proved important factors in eventually helping addicts become ex-addicts. This usually turned out not to be the case. None of the respondents reported strong untrammeled personal relationships which preexisted their addiction, were maintained throughout their addiction, and were instrumental in helping them stop use eventually. Instead, most of the addicts maintained troubled, dependent, and often guilt-ridden familial relationships during the major portions of their addiction career. They sought new and better families in the various treatment facilities onto whom they could transfer and eventually work out their childhood feelings. Only then were they free to form more meaningful personal relationships. Interestingly, even in these later relationships, the women appear as "mother-figures." For example, one ex-addict of twenty married a widow of forty-three with four children. In a number of patients, the element of testing-out the love of a parent proved an important factor however.

After asking respondents, "How did you stop using drugs?" we asked, "Who helped you?" None of the twenty-one survey respondents reported that he had been helped by a person who could be considered either a peer or a non-drug-related superior. The only help friends were reported to have offered was in directing them to a rehabilitation program.

Some addicts made it on their own without the benefit of any formal treatment program. We shall see that they, in fact, experienced different kinds of "treatment," some of them going to psychiatrists, others repeatedly experiencing detoxification, and still others going to prison, which it is possible to view as treatment in selected instances. In the case of one subject who had made it on his own, it emerged that he had worked at a variety of treatment facilities as a counselor and staff member. This became a means for helping or treating himself under the guise of helping others ("differential association").

Rehabilitative facilities thus symbolically represent the better family which can show concern for the addict and thus reach him. One of the addicts described the futility of detoxification since nobody seemed to care whether he made it or not. In fact, the staff actually anticipated failure so that there was no incentive to improve, and only a few did.

In one case, Mr. N. was helped by a girl friend to overcome feelings of inadequacy and fears of closeness. In the case of Mrs. B., the good mother in the form of the corrupt grandmother was the person who helped her. Mr. S. had a mother whom he need to test constantly; the fact that she stood by him through thick and thin was the major factor in his change. In the case of Mrs. B., she had been so burned and exploited by men that she could not form any male relationships. Her current adjustment as an ex-addict was based primarily on a phobic retreat from the world and a clinging to the home and babies as a sanctuary from which she feared to emerge.

An interesting fact crystallized in these studies is the intensely personal meaning different treatment facilities have for different addicts in terms of their previous lives. In the case of Mr. R., for example, we see that "family" was the predominant motif throughout his life, and the treatment facility which offered a warmer and more concerned family than his own was crucial in his making it. For I.R., Synanon became the better family; he was able to find a better father-figure to identify with in the person of Chuck Diedrich, the director. Respondents from other modalities describe the same experiences: Mr. C. and Mr. R., for example, used Pastor Rosado as a father-figure, and the church itself served as a warm and forgiving parental figure for subjects who had been deprived of both father and mother. They felt they had been stigmatized at birth, were bastards and orphans, and could only be redeemed by rebirth free of sin within the bosom of the Church.

ADDITIONAL "PULLS"

Description of Other Maladaptive Elements

Among other pulls which must be mentioned are the following:

1. The legitimate aspirations which were never lost sight of and which were reclaimed in the process of treatment. This is the concept of "two worlds." Many of the respondents never really lost sight of the square world and its values, and childhood goals; this later became a factor in their getting off drugs.

2. Another pull in treatment facilities is the possibility of upward social mobility by making it in a legitimate way. One of the powerful holds of Synanon, for example, is the system of rewards and punishment used. There are strong incentives for taking on responsibility with the support of the group, spurred on by the hope of eventually becoming a leader and running your own facility. This opportunity is also available through the Phoenix Houses and other residential centers. The recent burgeoning "profession" of ex-addicts offers graduates of a program the continued support of the treatment modality while they are helping others, in the sociological sense of "differential association."

Psychosocial Factors in the De-addiction Process

Psychological Components

In line with the usual descriptions of drug use as negative-destructive behavior, it is interesting to note how many of the respondents studied described a lack of security and emptiness, a search for love, and a father or mother figure, as the driving impulse of their lives. It was when someone went all out for them that treatment made a difference, as in the case of Pastor Rosado with Mr. C.; or when Mr. N.'s friend sold his coat to get him a fix.

While we did not have a chance to treat intensively most of the ex-addicts studied here (only one was thus engaged), we are aware of feelings of inadequacy and insecurity, confusion about psycho-sexual role, emptiness and depression; of secondary gains derived, and the negative attractions which made them so susceptible to the deviant culture. Very often, because of either the predominant influence of the mother or, conversely, the absence of a mother or father figure, the respondent needed to compensate through peer-group associations which became more important than the family. There are indications of sexual hangups and feelings of castration in a number of the men. We are also aware of self-destructive or, at least, self-defeating behavior, especially so in light of our society's criminal definition of the addiction problem. In one of the ex-addicts, clearly recognized death-wishes took the form of rescue fantasies: he was willing to play "Russian roulette" to the extent of risking his life to test and gain love and be saved. In the relationship with the parents, we often see a symbiosis with the mother; though, at times too, with the father. The fathers as role models mostly appear inadequate since they turn out to be alcoholics and, in the case of Mr. I.R.'s father, criminal and psychopathic as well, thus serving as distorted, impulsive, and deviant role models. More often, the fathers are absent, physically or emotionally, and play a small role in the child's rearing. In some cases, we find the family scapegoating one child, who is cast in the role of monster (clearly so in the case of I.R.) and becomes the victim of the family's hostile-destructive impulses. Others struggle with incestuous feelings to the mother and sometimes sisters. The destructive symbiosis is seen most clearly in the case of Mr. C., where the mother actually arranged to furnish drugs to her son for his own use or to sell. It is interesting how clear Mr. C. and I.R. are about the roles their mothers were playing and the lack of concern about them. The specific ways in which these factors interlaced with still others to become etiologic for drug use could probably be determined only through intensive therapy.

While we have focused exclusively on the role of the drugs themselves in the past, we can see more clearly how they serve to fulfill a number of needs basic to the psychic and social economy of the addict and homeostatic balance of the family as well. Their functions can be very varied. In the case of one addict, he at first didn't care so much about the drugs themselves, but used drugs to maintain contact with a friend who was very important in his life. In terms of sociological theories, we find corroboration of Walter Miller's culture-conflict theory in terms of the boys caught in a matriarchal family setup who seek reassurance about their masculinity in peer-group associations and establish their "machismo" by adopting hard values. This comes out in a number of the studies, as in Mr. R. and others. Much self-hatred and self-rejection is evident in many of the subjects, who feel themselves unacceptable and unlovable, bastards and sinners, and take drugs to relieve their self-hatred and block out feelings.

In regard to Merton's "status-frustration" theory, we see that a number of the addicts did have a desire for upward social mobility; and, surprisingly, were able to maintain their educational goals and middle-class values even while in jail. In terms of Merton's and Cloward and Ohlin's "differential access" theory, we saw that a number of the addicts identified with such role models as pimps or gangsters and adopted illegitimate means, since they did not feel the ordinary avenues were open to them. We are also interested in Cloward and Ohlin's "double-loser" theory that addicts are people who could not make it either by fighting or illegitimate means and chose drugs as a "retreatist" way out. This seems to be confirmed only in part. We have question about the word "retreatist," for example, since these addicts needed to be very active in maintaining their habit and learning all the rituals and effective means of supporting it. They were achieving their goals and needs through drug use and the drug life, apart from simply copping out or escaping;

and often never really relinquished their square goals. There are also various categories of addicts, including the hidden drug users, who are successful in conventional ways while using drugs.[3, 4] No uniform cover term can comprise the many different kinds of addicts to be found.

Sometimes psychological factors or problems are evidenced symbolically. These symbolic values later reappear as elements which helped a person to become de-addicted and rehabilitated. Mrs. B. for example, was caught between the image of "bad parents" and "good parents": the "bad parents" were the judges who were sure she was guility and were ready to condemn her to jail without a fair trial; and the "good parents" were the priest and the woman doctor who defended her and offered her a way out through the residential center. The situation is similarly clear in the case of L.S. who saw the judges as punishing fathers out to confirm his guilt and punish him. He fell back on sibling figures, namely the court attendants and police for support, but even they did not stand by him. He saw himself finally as a David pitted against Goliath, but it was clear that the odds were overwhelmingly against him, and he could not win. This sank in at the time of his long incarceration. There were other interesting aspects such as the symbolic castration of having his two small fingers removed, which may have helped relieve his guilt. The idea of castration is also evident in the case of Mr. R. when his brother died in jail. This aroused considerable guilt feeling in him and was a factor in his determination to get off drugs. In the case of others, we observe that they were infantilized in their nuclear families and never really weaned. Rehabilitation succeeded to the extent that it could provide kindly and firm parent figures to whom they could relate themselves. This comes out very clearly in the case of Synanon, the Damascus Church, and the methadone maintenance program.

RELATIONSHIP WITH PARENTS. In describing the conflictual family constellations of many of the subjects, the assumption is made that the problems originating here led many of the respondents to addiction. The cases cited here support the general feeling of troubled relationships with the parents. The classical literature on drug addiction describes a symbiotic relationship with the mother and a more distant, estranged relationship with the father, who may also be alcoholic or immature and impulse-ridden. At times, there may be a symbiotic tie with the father, as in the case of I.R. Instead of a symbiotic relationship with the mother, we may also note the loss of a mother figure, as in the case of Mr. N. and others, whose mothers died very early or were uninvolved so that they later searched for kindly mother persons as substitutes. At times, the mother is a hostile, witch-like figure and the person seeks a more loving mother, as in the case of I.R. On the other hand, some respondents could only begin rehabilitating themselves when their parents had cut them loose and they could no longer return to the home. An example of a symbiotic relationship with the father and son is evidenced by I.R., who felt "used" by the father as a feminine object and in competition with the mother for the father's attention. Some of this is also inherent in the case of Mr. N. who had a confused concept of his father, vacillating between the image of a very violent, strong figure and one who was also a sexual object and seductive with him.

REBELLION AND CONFORMITY. Though there is a stereotype that addicts are in rebellion against society and against their families, we often find that there are elements of conformity as well. As we saw, many of the parents of these addicts were themselves corrupt, immature, impulse-ridden, deviant, and alcoholic; and the addicts in these cases were therefore identifying with rather than rebelling against their parents. In the case of I.R., what appeared as a conventional, middle-class, Italian family was rather the prototype for I.R.'s deviant behavior since the father was himself a criminal, shylock, blackmailer, and heavy drinker. The mother of Mr. C. was herself corrupt and tried to share in his drug-selling activities and profit by them. On the other hand, we very often do note rebellion against square values. The fact is that they find it much harder to adapt to a square culture and easier to relate to deviant activities and the drug culture, no matter how terrible the consequences. A number of the addicts studied maintained their square ideals even through the worst periods of their addicted life.

ACTING-OUT BEHAVIOR. Many of the addicts were plagued by

feelings of anxiety and depression. For various reasons, they could not internalize their conflicts, but resolved them through acting-out behavior, for the most part antisocially. As I.R. made clear, he tried to block out "my parents' insanity"; and, in fact, repressed all feelings in himself by acting out his problems. It was not until he was nineteen and had arrived in Synanon that he first began to understand what feelings were and learned to deal with them.

GUILT AND SELF-PUNISHMENT. A recurrent element is that of guilt and self-punishment. We see this clearly in the case of Mrs. A. who was troubled by the fact that she had six children, one of them mentally retarded, for which she blamed herself, believing she had damaged the fetus through her use of barbiturates and amphetamines. She felt inadequate in relation to her mother, who had been able to conceive and take care of twelve children, whereas Mrs. A. could not take care of any of her own. There was therefore competition with the mother, guilt over the neglect of the children and the destruction of one child. We often assume the existence of guilt even if it is not clearly evident by virtue of the fact that being part of the drug culture is in time destructive for most addicts, leading to increasing punishment, imprisonment, and often death. This comes out in the O.D.'s where the men wish to die and resent being revived by other people.

In the case of Mrs. A., the existence of masochism is apparent since she allowed herself to be exploited by her husband and his friends, prostituted for them, and turned over all her money to them so that they could shoot drugs. She had been so "burned" and became so mistrustful that she could no longer relate to men.

QUESTIONS OF MASCULINITY; CASTRATION FEELINGS. We note that many of the men had severe sexual problems, many being troubled by the feeling that their penis was too small (a frequent symbol of inferiority feelings), concern about premature ejaculation, and fears of women, among others. One subject, not discussed here, consciously resorted to drugs to "cop out" (escape) because he felt he couldn't handle sex adequately, and only learned to do this after the Synanon experience. Another subject was similarly concerned about his small penis, and, for many years, could not urinate in a public place where other men congregated (related to sexual rivalry with the father). Some of the sexual problems are related to incestuous problems, as in one case where the mother was so openly seductive and both parents so exhibitionist that the subject still cannot relate freely to women. To prove "manliness," the men often had tattoos on their arms or hands, representing the pacheco symbol or other signs of machismo and toughness. In one case, the search for peer-group identification and manliness through association with ghetto blacks was especially clear. The subject vacillated between middle-class and lower-class values and was very aware of color differences since his grandparents were darker and his mother lighter. He lived in a matriarchal household and had no masculine figure to emulate except for an emasculated grandfather and absent father. His attendance at an enlightened private school further confused him in relation to his own values and identity. He tried to resolve this by becoming a ghetto black person where he could finally believe that he "belonged" by falling to the bottom of the totem pole in the Harlem ghetto.

COUNTERPHOBIC MECHANISM. As part of the testing-out of masculinity and adequacy, mention must generally be made of the "counterphobic mechanism," that is, the need to expose oneself to feared situations in order to prove oneself. At times, drugs were themselves personalized ambivalently in the sense that they were needed, yet appeared as an opponent to be confronted and conquered. Many addicts never believed they could become addicted. It was only after they had become hooked that they realized they had "lost." This reinforces Lindesmith's concept of the recognition of one's addiction and withdrawal distress as an important element in developing the image of an addict.[5]

FEARS OF CLOSENESS. Drug use often involves fears of closeness and is used as a device for keeping people at a distance, avoiding exposure of the need to share feelings and to give of oneself. Through drugs, one can immunize oneself against the world, avoid pain, stress, and the need to feel. This is clearly evidenced in the case of Mr. R. and others.

BOREDOM. "Boredom" is a word commonly used by addicts. They become restless and need to run and be active, usually in their drug and other antisocial activities. It is a cover word for emptiness, anxiety, depression, and the need to act out to deal with tensions, as well as deny and block out feelings and awareness.

EGO MASTERY. Ego mastery has both psychological and social components. The idea of "cool" or "hip" has already been discussed in relation to ego mastery and fear of loss of control.

THE NEED TO BELONG. The need to belong, often with older companions, is an important element. I.R. initially wanted to be accepted by an older crowd, and drug use became one method for being accepted by this group. Before he actually used himself, he would hold the tourniquets and help the older boys inject themselves (which had overtones of homosexual activity). Before R. was a seasoned musician, he could be accepted by established musicians on the basis of their mutual drug use.

FEAR OF SUCCESS. An element not yet mentioned is the frequent fear of assuming responsibility and succeeding. Mr. R. used drugs as a cop-out from competition, which he feared.

Drug use can nevertheless become a means of making it, at least briefly, through illegitimate means. In the long run, you must almost invariably lose out. Many addicts tattoo the pacheco symbol on their hands, which represents being a "loner" and a "loser." Although lower-class addicts may temporarily feel they are making it by earning large sums of money by wheeling and dealing, they discover in time that all the money goes down the drain through the needle, and there is no percentage. This is also true of women who prostitute.

Sociological Aspects

EXHAUSTION OF RESOURCES. The addictive life is exhausting in all respects—personal and material. We can imagine the physical wear and tear of being constantly on the go to hustle money for drugs, seek out connections, avoid detection and arrest, go to jails and hospitals. A terrible grinding down of the person results to the point where he loses track of time, and all events are telescoped so that he later finds it difficult to recapitulate his history and chronology. In the case of I.R., we saw that he had made himself *persona non grata* to all the hospitals in New York by his provocative behavior. His family was similarly tired and refused to admit him. The shylocks were out hunting for him, and the police, too, were looking. A number of dramatic and dangerous events converged toward the end, entailing narrow escapes from death, seeing a friend shot and presumably killed by a policeman, and others. Fortunately, he was able to get to a Synanon facility in time.

THE TESTING OF FATE. There appear to be strong elements of a gambling addiction in drug addiction, since many addicts try to see how far they can go in attempting to defy fate. One patient had the rescue fantasy that by O.D.'ing he could learn whether people loved him enough to rescue him when he was on the verge of death. The subjects were ready to risk all to wrench an answer from fate, "Am I or am I not lovable?"

In the case of others, they came to a final desperate point of seeming to stake all on a last gamble. This was especially clear in the cases of Mr. C. and Mr. N. who decided, under impossible odds, to steal a large sum of money and set themselves straight. One of them had a hand grenade, and the other was ready to barge impulsively into a jewelry store. At the last moment, they were dissuaded by friends, and this became a proof of love and concern. A friend gave Mr. C. the coat off his back for a fix, and this constituted the turning point for him.

FADING OF INITIAL GLAMOUR OF USE. Whatever kicks and glamour adhered to the "honeymoon" period of use were outweighed by the burden of being an addict twenty-four hours a day. In looking back, many of the addicts saw their life as indescribable, terrible, and themselves as zombies and "living deaths." The possibility of being able to clean up their lives again looms strongly in their quest for help.

THE CONCEPT OF "ROCK BOTTOM." The concept of "rock bottom," as discussed previously, is a most interesting one since the addicts in many cases appeared to have reached rock bottom, a point of no return, while others did not, thus demonstrating

the subjective or relative nature of what constitutes this point
for different addicts. For many, life became intolerable, and
they could not continue any longer. Some of the addicts experienced a number of O.D.'s, narrowly escaped death a number of
times, and actively yearned for death. Mrs. B. had been so
severely beaten by the police that she required hospitalization:
she was suffering from toxemia, was pregnant again, debilitated,
and had exhausted all resources. It was only through the strong
intervention of friends such as the priest and the woman doctor
at Bellevue that she finally found an exit in the structured
environment of a therapeutic community. In the case of another
addict, rock bottom was quite subjective, coming very early
when he discovered that being an addict meant losing his
middle-class status and his savings. Upward social mobility was
the guiding *leitmotif* in his life. Since he could not make it
through drug use, he was going to dissociate himself from it.
He was also doing other things which were intolerable to him,
such as beating a woman for money and abusing his father, from
whom he had always sought approval.

THE "MATURING-OUT" CONCEPT. Regarding rock bottom, it
must be pointed out that a number of addicts were de-addicted
at a relatively early age; surprisingly so, in light of the maturing-
out theory which postulates that addicts usually start growing
out of drug use in their late twenties and thirties. Some young
subjects actually stopped by the age of nineteen, and others
were ready to change and make it in the early twenties. An
important parameter here was the availability of far better
treatment resources than in past years, which afforded an exit
from the addiction system when the men were ready to stop.
It is possible to see in better perspective that the reason why
one needed to wait so long in the fifties and sixties was that there
were few effective treatment modalities on hand. It should be
added that many had also begun use far earlier than previously
believed—at ages twelve or thirteen. There is evidence from
various follow-up studies of increasing abstinence in the populations studied as time goes on.[17, 22] While there has been much
conjecture about the reason or reasons for this, including elaborate
metabolic theories, a more obvious finding supported by these

studies relates to the increasing maladaptiveness of the addictive life as time goes on.

LIFE AS AN EX-ADDICT. Most of the ex-addicts were selective as to whom they revealed they had been heroin users. Of the twenty-one survey respondents for whom we have information, six were secretive and did not want anyone to know about their addiction. Nine did not mind some people's knowing, but wished the information restricted. Only five of the twenty-one wanted people to know they were addicts. All of the latter were participants in religious programs and wished to "testify" that they had been saved by God so that they might more effectively do God's work by helping cure other addicts. The fact that such a large proportion of ex-addicts working in the addiction field wanted to keep their former addiction at least partially secret suggests the difficulty researchers may have in reaching and interviewing ex-addicts not affiliated with a program.

Only a minority of the ex-addicts had stable marital relations. Four were married prior to, or during their addiction and are still married. Nine of the other twenty-seven married or re-married since abstaining from heroin. Eighteen of the thirty-one are presently unmarried. Of these, eight had never been married, and eight were divorced or separated prior to abstaining. Although a fairly high proportion of the ex-addicts are married, the majority are not. They thus exhibit the same lack of strong, enduring relationships common to addicts.

We did not make a comprehensive effort to measure the social or psychological adjustment of our thirty-one ex-addicts. All were functioning fairly normally and, as noted, most were regularly employed. They would still be considered to have problems, but whether these problems are more serious than those of people from similar backgrounds is not clear. This question is most important in judging the adjustment of ex-addicts in terms of social functioning or drug use: How does their adjustment compare with the typical adjustment of the general population from which they derive?

VALIDITY OF LIFE CYCLE MODEL. The life cycle model used as the prime parameter for this study was based on extensive data as to how certain people become street addicts, and from this were extrapolated the processes by which addicts would most likely grow out. The model is only a rough outline, however, and is not meant to imply a smooth progression from stage to stage. For example, there may be regressive movements back and forth at any point rather than the smooth progression indicated in the model or an indefinite plateau. Not every patient may be rehabilitated even if his drug use becomes highly maladaptive and stressful. Many addicts die or kill themselves. Others achieve great competence in functioning within the system or else have access to money, which relieves much of the hardship inherent in copping to support the habit. Still others are hidden drug addicts who are conventional in all areas of living—work and home—except for their drug use.[9]

The author had initially disapproved of addicts' remaining in the addiction system, i.e. working within their treatment program as "professional ex-addicts" in order to help others. He now believes it important that many ex-addicts remain within the system since this reinforces their own rehabilitation and growth in the sense of differential association through the constant support of the facility and the reinforcements derived from helping others.

VALUE OF TYPOLOGIES. Our detailed studies show that the different typologies are useful for purposes of general rough classification, but can become Procrustean beds if adhered to too closely since no one typology can fully encompass the totality of an individual's actual life experience. The typologies can help us understand certain aspects of an addict's career, but can be mutually supplementary since they highlight different aspects of the addict career—somewhat like the parable of the three blind men describing an elephant.

UTILITY OF VARIOUS SOCIOLOGICAL THEORIES. The life histories appear to corroborate the various sociological theories discussed at the beginning of this volume:

Walter Miller's "cultural conflict" theory. Drug use constitutes for addicts the means for rejecting the square society and achieving feelings of belonging by adopting deviant role models and the addict tribal culture with all its rituals and associations.

In some minority cultures, drug use constitutes part of a peer-group reinforcement of male values ("machismo").[23]

Merton's "status-frustration" theory. Deviant activities and dealing with drugs, if not drug use itself, seem to offer lower-class individuals the opportunity for achieving success through illegitimate means. In the early "honeymoon" stage, they had more money than ever before through "dealing" and other deviant activities. Many of the ex-addicts used gangsters and pimps as their early role models. In the long run, however, the drug life inevitably defeated their upward mobility—a fact well known to addicts who tattoo the phrase "born to lose" on their arms and hands.[3]

Cloward and Ohlin's "differential access" theory. Cloward and Ohlin described addicts as *double failures* since they could make it by neither legitimate means ("bopping") nor by criminal behavior. Actually, addicts can often be very aggressive and become extremely proficient in stealing and dealing, but any gain is lost through their use of drugs in the end. A serious mistake of Cloward and Ohlin is their stereotyping of addicts as if they were all alike. As mentioned, there are many kinds of addicts and drug abusers from different ethnic, class, and geographical backgrounds with varying degrees of involvement in the addiction system. Some achieve considerable competence in their drug use and are never detected, while others may be totally engulfed. The hidden drug abusers located in the Bronx were never arrested or even hospitalized and were successful in the conventional world.

The goals of addicts are indeed *retreatist* from those of our general society, but the actual facts are far more complicated. Many addicts never lose sight of their square goals and may be trying to achieve them through deviant means. As indicated, such retained square values may become an important factor in their later growing out of the addiction system.[4]

Lindesmith postulated that it was recognition of one's addiction and withdrawal distress which became the primary factors in shaping an addict. While this has been confirmed as an important element, it is only *one* among a number of factors. Lindesmith didn't account for the fact that some addicts may drop out at this point and also that further progressions need to occur if one decides to remain an addict—such as developing the self-image of a junkie, learning the rituals of copping, shooting, "hustling," and others.[5]

No striking variations in psychological and social factors were observed in disparate representatives from different classes or cultures as diverse as Cuban, Puerto Rican, black, Jewish, Italian, It has been conjectured that middle-class patients have more psychological hang-ups than lower-class patients since they have access to opportunity for upward mobility yet eschew these and seek the bottom. They may later respond more readily to treatment facilities involving encounters, intellectualization and "games," and the development of insight. Lower-class addicts have proven less responsive to the approaches of the ex-addict-directed therapeutic communities, and more so to modalities where physical or religious approaches are emphasized, such as methadone maintenance, the former Damascus Christian Church, and Teen Challenge.

Though distinct variations were noted in the overt and covert philosophy and practices of the various treatment modalities, it would be useful to gather further data on this point. The author's own rationale calls for a multimodality approach to treatment with research and evaluation built in to determine what approach works for what kind of addict.[24, 25]

VII

CURRENT TRENDS IN DRUG ABUSE: PROBLEMS AND MANAGEMENT

THIS CHAPTER IS intended to complete our discussion of prevailing treatment approaches and the issues involved in each, and to detail current trends in the newly-emerging forms of drug abuse and outline suggested treatment approaches for dealing with them.[26-28]

Each society has its own "Gestalt" and establishes its institutions and shibboleths accordingly. It decides which drugs it likes or dislikes and which can and cannot serve a role in its own culture. This will vary from society to society. The story is often told that when coffee first became popular in the East, it was condemned as the devil's brew, and everything possible was done to suppress its use. Its sale was prohibited, and stacks of coffee were destroyed wherever found. Individuals convicted of drinking coffee were led through town mounted on donkeys, and its use was declared contrary to the spirit of the Koran. All this, of course, only made people more interested in coffee, and its use spread steadily. Finally, all the laws needed to be repealed; and the pendulum swung so far in the opposite direction that a new Turkish law was passed stipulating that refusal of a husband to give his wife coffee was legal grounds for divorce.[29]

This story underlines a point: our society defined heroin and opiate use as a criminal problem and consequently forced such users into the criminal subculture. On the other hand, we have been far less concerned with drugs which are more pervasive and serious in terms of body effects—such as the so-called "soft drugs"—amphetamines, barbiturates, and the hallucinogens. We were also, until recently, quite cavalier about tobacco; nor are we still sufficiently alarmed about the prevalence of serious alcoholism.

CHANGING OUR PERSPECTIVE

This section will summarize the drug abuse situation as it existed until recently, and then describe new developments and changes. Very briefly, the classical picture of the heroin addict for whom the drug of choice was heroin ninety-one percent of the time and who used other drugs primarily to "boost" or potentiate the effects of his heroin, has changed. There is now a "new breed" of young multiple drug users who are abusing a variety of drugs simultaneously—amphetamines, barbiturates, tranquilizers, sedative-hypnotics such as Doriden, as well as alcohol and narcotics, and who may be addicted to one or more of these drugs simultaneously. There is thus a "cultural lag" in our understanding of the current scene, and it is timely that we correct our perspective.

To add to this picture, the age of drug abusers has been dropping steadily so that we now find heroin users ten years old and younger. The problem of non-opiate abuse is compounded by the fact that it comprises at least two distinct groups: those who are using drugs within a conventional-legal-medical context as a means of maximizing their functioning and achieving conventional social goals; and the younger "cultogenic," spree abusers who are using drugs illicitly to meet sociopathic or "deviant" goals. While our criminal definition of the heroin problem permitted a clear demarcation between heroin addicts and conventional persons, the distinctions in other psychotropic drugs, including barbiturates, amphetamines, hallucinogens, sedative-hypnotics, tranquilizers, and a host of the newer drugs, are not nearly as clear. It is important that these variations be kept in mind in any consideration of the drug problem today.

More research is required to understand the etiology of soft drug abuse and the progressions from non-use to experimentation to heavier involvement and addiction. An important caveat, also, is the need to avoid "universalization" and, consequently, hysteria by constantly citing the high numbers of users or abusers involved. It is essential that we begin sorting out those using drugs in a legal-medical context from the illicit users; and to sift out also the infrequent abusers from the heavily involved, who should be the main target of our treatment interventions.

THE TREATMENT OF NARCOTIC ADDICTION

This section will summarize briefly the major modalities for the treatment of narcotic addiction which have evolved in recent years.

Until recently, it was generally acknowledged that the field of rehabilitation of narcotic addicts had been characterized far more by failure than success. Workers in this area had little hope of achieving successful treatment which would enable addicts to avoid relapse to drugs. The harshness of our laws as they applied to narcotics possession, superimposed upon the complex psychosocial problems of addicts and the confusion as to suitable goals of treatment, confronted treatment personnel with the difficult task of rendering addicts totally and immediately abstinent.

In examining the variety of treatment methods or modalities currently employed to deal with this problem, we find it possible to categorize them as follows: punitive, medical-psychiatric, communal (Synanon, Phoenix, etc.) religious, the use of rational authority, and chemotherapy (cyclazocine and methadone maintenance). Since it is possible to present only very brief descriptions of the major modalities here, the reader is referred to other writings of the author for more detailed discussions.[21, 24, 30-33]

Punitive Approach

Because of the many laws which make it a crime to sell, purchase, or possess without a legitimate medical prescription, those drugs classified by the World Health Organization as "dangerous drugs," or even to possess a hyperdermic syringe unless medically prescribed, addicts are for the most part compelled to seek out illicit sources of drugs for which exorbitant prices are demanded. A criminal pattern of "hustling" for money and drugs is generally soon developed. Under this system, almost all addicts become criminals and are imprisoned for varying periods of time.

It is possible to argue that the imprisonment of addicts is a form of treatment, in that it may serve as a deterrent against further criminal acts and as punishment for the commission of the crime, and may even help addicts pause to reflect on their acting-out behavior. This punitive "modality" has been the most extensive "treatment" offered addicts since the early twenties, and all efforts to rehabilitate have been geared to the existing framework of the law and definition of the problem. This approach has been modified by the author to the concept of "rational authority" discussed in a later section.

Medical

Concurrent with this traditional approach, though gaining momentum later, was the emergence of the medical setting, at times buttressed by limited psychiatric services and the recognition that narcotics addiction needed to be viewed as an "illness." In the thirties, the United States Public Health Service established two federal hospitals, one in Lexington, Kentucky and the other in Fort Worth, Texas. The treatment emphases developed at these hospitals were later carried over to facilities in New York City such as the Riverside Hospital, Manhattan State, and "detoxification hospitals" such as Metropolitan and Manhattan General Hospital (the Morris Bernstein Institute of Beth Israel Hospital). Recent findings by Martin et al. regarding the "protracted abstinence syndrome," i.e. that the physical effects of sustained opioid abuse can last as long as seven months, indicate the need for longer periods of care to effect detoxification.[10]

Essentially, the treatment procedures in these settings consisted of detoxification with adjuvant services, including a physical workup and some rebuilding of physical health, limited counseling, and welfare assistance services. There was minimal emphasis on aftercare help once the patient left the hospital.

These two treatment approaches, the punitive and the medical hospital setting, have been viewed by many as gross failure since they did not appear to prevent addicts' relapse to drugs nor alter their addictive life style. This approach has been changed drastically, with primary emphasis placed on aftercare help in the local community rather than in isolated institutions. Ambulatory detox is used in some hospitals in New York and Philadelphia, and methadone stabilization on an ambulatory basis is the preferred method in the majority of cases today in New York and elsewhere.

Communal Approach—The Ex-addict-directed Therapeutic Communities

Within the last decade, there emerged a number of new treatment modalities based on different assumptions and stressing other themes of rehabilitation. The most highly publicized of these was the "communal," best illustrated by Synanon, Daytop Village, and more recently by other therapeutic communities carrying out the "concept" and bearing such names as "Phoenix House," "Odyssey House," and others.

These approaches are predicated on placing the addict in a twenty-four-hour residential setting directed by ex-addicts who serve as role models. Through group encounters and seminars, "stews" and marathons, the addict's values and way of life are questioned intensively. The closeness achieved has been described as that of the "extended family" with a system of rewards and punishments built in as a means of social control. While these approaches have been effective for some addicts, a relevant criticism has been their failure to return more than a very small number of residents rehabilitated to the community. There has been increasing question about the need to use the humiliation and hazing techniques and the stripping of defenses comprised under the "concept"—especially with addicts and members of minority groups who have already been severely traumatized. Greater emphasis needs to be placed on "reentry" efforts, on overcoming the phobic stance to other approaches, and cooperating with hitherto rejected modalities such as the chemotherapy approaches or "rational authority" in order to enhance their effectiveness.[31, 33]

Religious Approach

This approach can be demonstrated most dramatically in the work of the former Damascus Christian Church in the South

Bronx and, currently in the work of Teen Challenge in Brooklyn, California, and other areas. In this modality, addiction, alcoholism, and other deviant behavior are viewed not so much as a sickness, crime, or even social phenomenon, as a "sin." The Fundamentalist Pentecostal religious orientation provides an intensive religious experience and group supports for those willing to accept salvation by embracing Christ and the Church. He who was lowest can become highest, since one can become a minister of the Church. It is obvious that not all addicts can respond to such missionary zeal or develop the deep religious conviction required; over 80 percent drop out in the first two weeks. The Damascus Church approach appears to have been especially effective with Puerto Ricans in the Bronx area. The Black Muslims have similarly been able to convert and help black addicts, but because of their inordinately high standards, only a few have been able to meet their austere requirements.[24, 30, 33] Teen Challenge has been able to help a small number, but needs to develop better treatment techniques and modes of "reentry," as well as evaluation components.

Rational Authority

Rational authority, a concept derived from Fromm and Weber, was visualized by the author as an instrument for providing a firm structuring of the treatment relationship, including the setting of limits, controls, and sanctions through which the acting-out behavior of addicts could be curbed. This approach was studied at the Washington Heights Rehabilitation Center administered by the author from 1962 to 1967 under the aegis of the National Institute of Mental Health-New York City Department of Health and New York City Office of Probation.

The relationship between the center and the probation office was unique in that no "confidentiality" was observed in line with the usual secrecy maintained between community agencies and probation and parole. The center's information was shared with the probation office, as was planning and joint decision-making. The patient did not feel he could manipulate one agency against another to satisfy his own impulsive needs as he formerly did with his parents. The program was also unique in setting the use of authority at the center of the program as a subject of study. The program and its findings are discussed at length in the book *Authority and Addiction*. The program was the forerunner of a number of civil commitment programs such as those of California, New York State, and most recently, the Federal Narcotic Addiction Rehabilitation Administration (NARA). Rational authority can be used as a structuring technique and reinforcement in any treatment modality.[24, 30]

Cyclazocine

Martin and his co-workers at the United States Public Health Service Hospital in Lexington, Kentucky had earlier proposed that the regular administration of cyclazocine, a long-acting narcotics antagonist in the benzomorphan series, might be useful in the treatment of highly motivated ambulatory patients to avoid relapse to the compulsive use of narcotics.[34]

Even with the limitations of a drug that must be taken daily, the cyclazocine studies demonstrated that some compulsive narcotics users do have considerable motivation to become abstinent and, in some cases, can do this without prolonged hospitalization. It was found that cyclazocine, in and of itself, could not effect rehabilitation and that individual and group counseling services needed to be built in as well. Cyclazocine thus served as a lever in therapy: by stabilizing patients and blocking the effects of their drug use, extinction of prior conditioning to heroin use could result and the process of rehabilitation be rendered more rapid and efficient. Conceivably, cyclazocine and other narcotics antagonists may eventually find wide application with neophyte or long-term motivated users, as well as in reinforcing the goals of probation. At present, it seems to fill an important gap in the therapeutic armamentarium and can be of value for individuals who are not ready to concede their need for long-term in-patient treatment or for ambulatory maintenance on synthetic narcotics such as methadone. Work has also been done with a later drug, naloxone, which has some advantages and some deficits. Further research needs to be undertaken to develop longer-acting forms and determine the particular segments of the drug population for whom they are suitable.[24, 30, 32] This research is increasingly being pursued.

Methadone Maintenance

Among the most important research under way in this country at the present time is the study of the use of methadone in the social rehabilitation of chronic, compulsive heroin users. By far the largest and most thorough study was that begun in 1963 by Dole and Nyswander at the Rockefeller Institute, which is now being replicated in various parts of the city, country, and abroad. Recent evaluations by the Columbia School of Public Health indicate it to be helping the majority of their patients.[24, 35]

It was early apparent that methadone, used appropriately, had all the characteristics required for a drug of stabilization. Furthermore, when patients were given extremely large doses of methadone, one additional effect is obtained: a remarkable degree of tolerance to methadone itself and all other opiate-like drugs is induced. It is worth noting that, in this respect, the effect of methadone is somewhat similar to that of cyclazocine. The repeated ineffectual use of heroin could conceivably result in a gradual extinction of instrumentally reinforced heroin-seeking behavior. In the Dole-Nyswander program, the over-whelming majority of patients showed dramatic changes in social behavior and became self-supporting, many for the first time in their lives.

A number of innovations have been undertaken, including the stabilization of patients on an ambulatory basis, combining methadone with a therapeutic community for the more recalcitrant patients, randomizing the selection of patients, use of urinalysis, and others. The multiple possible use of methadone in a gradient from simple to complex for different kinds of methadone patients has been described by the author in recent papers.[25, 35]

While methadone has established itself as the most effective modality for large groups of addicts, much more research needs to be undertaken, such as the optimal structuring of treatment for different kinds of patients, studying dose-curve relationships, short- and long-term effects of use, and others. It is important, for example, that the program continue to be firmly structured and that efforts be made to learn the different services required for different kinds of methadone patients, including also the feasibility of getting large numbers off in time. While there has been talk also of dispensing with urine testing, it seems most important that this be continued for treatment and research purposes, especially so because of the large amount of "cheating" described in some recent studies. The significance of this "cheating" needs to be investigated further.[36] Another question is, How shall we deal with the new multiple drug users only incidentally involved with heroin?

There has also been increasing question about many of the concepts advanced, such as "narcotic blockade," and this too needs to be researched. If there is indeed a blockade, why do addicts still feel a "buzz" with relatively small amounts of methadone, and why can some patients make it on low-dose methadone without the blockade?

Though the Gearing evaluations have demonstrated abundantly that the social productivity of methadone patients is increased, we still do not know the actual quality of their work performance and interpersonal relationships, or the short- and long-term effects of methadone. Some of the program directors have seized on methadone as a new toy and do not appear to understand the complex problems of the addict which remain to be dealt with even with the use of chemotherapy. More thorough-going evaluation and research are urgently called for in all these areas.[33, 35]

A Multimodality Approach to Treatment

In recent years, the author has advocated a multimodality approach to the treatment of heroin use generally, among other reasons, as a means of heading off the internecine rivalry and extravagant claims of success of the various drug treatment agencies. In brief, the multimodality rationale emanates from the belief that there is no such universal as "the addict," but rather a variety of addicts with different social and psychological characteristics, of varying ages, ethnic and class backgrounds, stages of involvement in the addiction system, and states of readiness for help. By building in evaluation to determine what characteristics lend themselves to help under particular treatment modalities, it is hoped to develop objective criteria for the screening and treatment of patients. Thus, after an initial interview, patients could be referred to the modality best equipped to help them—whether a residential center, religious approach, the narcotics-antagonist cyclazocine, methadone maintenance, or any other program or even combination of programs—either to reinforce treatment or cover different stages of treatment.[21]

THE PROBLEM OF NON-OPIATE ABUSE

There has been no determination of the prevalence of non-narcotic drug abusers in the United States, nor do we have the means for ascertaining how many of the legally manufactured and distributed drugs find their way into the illicit market. Independent figures and estimates indicate that this abuse is widespread and that there is a constant supply of non-narcotic drugs in the illicit market.

Two general facts about the current abuse of the non-narcotic drugs—amphetamines, barbiturate-sedatives, and tranquilizers—emerge from the available patchwork of figures and estimates. First, amphetamines appear to be more widely abused than the barbiturate-sedatives, and the barbiturate-sedatives more widely than tranquilizers. Second, of the three classes of drugs, the barbiturate-sedatives appear to inflict the most damage on the abuser's health and conventional functioning. As also mentioned earlier, the newer users are abusing a wide variety of drugs, whatever they can obtain readily, and may be addicted to one or more of these drugs at any given time.[26]

The following section will describe the non-opiate drugs generally and then offer brief discussions of treatment. Since special approaches still need to be devised for the treatment of non-opiate abuse, the paper will conclude with the author's suggestions for indicated modalities.

Barbiturates

While the barbiturates were believed to be capable of producing a psychic dependence (habituation), it took nearly half a century to convince the practicers of clinical medicine that they were indeed drugs of addiction if abused. Even with indisputable evidence of the addiction liability of the drugs, they did not come under effective control by the Federal Government until the mid-1960's.

As with narcotic addicts and alcoholics, barbiturate abusers, regardless of type, may not ordinarily seek treatment until such time as their abuse has precipitated some crisis, e.g. the loss of a job, marital difficulty, a police contact, the loss of a drug supply, etc. If an addicted barbiturate abuser does seek treatment, or if it is imposed, the detoxification phase of treatment should occur on an inpatient basis since it can be life-threatening.[37]

The contraindication of abrupt withdrawal of barbiturates and the specific symptoms to expect from physically dependent persons are widely documented in the literature. A majority of the patients may experience coma, convulsions, and the equivalent of the D.T.'s unless extreme caution is observed. Even a rapid reduction of the dose to which the person has become tolerant is considered dangerous. The general procedure for the medically controlled withdrawal process dates to the pioneering work done by Isbell and his associates in 1950.[38] If the barbiturate abuser has concurrently abused other drugs which require a separate withdrawal regimen, the evidence is that multiple withdrawals can be conducted simultaneously without increasing the problem of abstinence from either.

The literature indicates further that once primary withdrawal has been completed—in two to three weeks—the rehabilitative and psychotherapeutic treatment of the barbiturate abuser resembles that of the narcotic addict. It has been the author's experience that high-frequency, individual supportive counseling is a valuable procedure during the initial abstinence phase of treatment, with the main therapeutic emphasis on the acquisition or sharpening of coping skills. While these abusers are more likely to have more competitive skills, e.g. education, jobs, status, intact families, than the narcotic abusers, they seem to be deficient in their ability to adapt and adjust to new or stressful situations. While it is possible to foster and enhance these coping skills in group settings, individual sessions are probably more appropriate for initiating the process. Once some minimal insight and progress are achieved, the group setting where testing can occur and be analyzed is usually indicated.

Barbiturate abuse is best viewed as a chronic relapsing disease. Contact should therefore be maintained with the ex-abuser for an extended period of time. While our experience is somewhat limited in this area, the management of patients during this extended "aftercare" phase may be effectively accomplished in regular, if infrequent group sessions. Groups with enduring histories appear most appropriate for the rapid discovery of anxieties or depression, which too frequently signal relapse in these patients. Both multiple-diagnoses groups, as well as groups comprised only of barbiturate abusers have produced favorable results. Neither has been rigorously studied for measures of outcome, however.[38]

Non-barbiturate Sedative-hypnotic Abusers

Several of the newer nonbarbiturate sedative-hypnotic drugs, when abused, have been shown to produce intoxication, dependence, coma, and/or death resembling those due to barbiturate abuse. They include drugs under the generic and brand names of meprobamate (Miltown, Equanil, etc.), glutethimide (Doriden), ethinamate (Valmid), ethchlorvynol (Placidyl), methpyrylon (Noludar), chlordiazepoxide (Librium), diazepam (Valium), oxazepam (Serax).

While these drugs are indeed addicting if misused, the available evidence would suggest this addiction will occur only at dose levels considerably in excess of those therapeutically prescribed. Though our experience in treating nonbarbiturate sedative-hypnotic abusers is too limited to permit generalization, we would expect the treatment process to parallel the three treatment phases which have been effective with barbiturate abusers: the initial detoxification, initial abstinence, and extended aftercare.

Specific research still needs to be conducted to validate the therapeutic techniques most appropriate for different types of abusers. While we are acutely aware that therapeutic success, regardless of the technique, is intimately related to the skills of the therapist, it should be possible at some future date to predict, with a greater degree of success, which patients will relapse and why, and the techniques to be used to obviate this.[26]

Amphetamine Abusers

Amphetamine abusers appear to fall into two somewhat distinct contrasting types. Obviously, such a dichotomous characterization of amphetamine abusers cannot be totally distinct since there are many gradations and exceptions. Still, it does provide an appropriate framework within which to provide treatment services. We have chosen to label these two types of abusers *adaptive* and *escapist*.

The *adaptive abusers* may be characterized generally as using amphetamines to bolster their functioning in conventional interpersonal and social activities. This type of abuser tends to deny abuse upon initial confrontation, and, when the denial is no longer possible, will contend the drugs prevent or eliminate "problems" rather than cause them. The adaptive abuser has usually enjoyed some success in his interactions and social competitiveness, but mistakenly believes that the drug permits him to recapture or increase this success. In contrast, the *escapist abusers* may be generically characterized as using drugs *not* to function within a conventional interpersonal and social framework. They do not tend to deny the abuse when confronted but have ready multiple rationalizations as to why it occurs. They have not normally enjoyed much success in their interactions and social competitiveness and escape through their use of drugs.

Amphetamine abusers of the escapist type characteristically abuse their drugs in a cycle. The cycle has two basic phases: an *up* or active phase and a *down* or reactive phase. The two phases are approximately equal in duration. Typically, an experienced abuser would inject the drug, usually methamphetamine, at two- to four-hour intervals for four or five days (the action phase), during which time he will remain awake continuously and then collapse from exhaustion and remain in a semicomatose state, sleeping intermittently for the next four or five days.

Regarding treatment, the initial "detoxification" phase of treament is basically a medical process and should be accomplished on an inpatient basis. While there is apparently no harm in the abrupt withdrawal of amphetamines since they are not considered physically addicting in the sense of heroin or barbiturates, the psychiatric reactions to amphetamine abuse, which reportedly range from acute anxiety to full-blown psychosis, may often require medication, e.g. sedatives or phenothiazine. Concurrent medical problems associated with the intravenous high-dose abusers may also require attention during this phase of treatment.[26]

Amphetamine abusers of the adaptive type *should not* be treated in proximity with the escapist type of amphetamine abusers or most narcotic addicts. It would appear appropriate to treat them in proximity with other "medicine abusers," e.g. abusers of tranquilizers, antidepressants, and some analgesic addicts who had medical or accidental onsets. Clinicians must be constantly alert to the possibility of a multidependent patient.

The author believes that the treatment of amphetamine abusers, regardless of type, should include the same general phases as with barbiturate users: an initial physiological detoxification phase, initial abstinent phase, and long-term aftercare phase. Advocating these three phases is based more upon preliminary clinical deductions than extensive clinical experience, but with the aim of providing an appropriate framework within which experience can be accumulated.

The initial detoxification phase can be completed within one week. Even though there is evidence that portions of the primary withdrawal distress may continue for several weeks, it is recommended that the second phase of treatment—initial abstinence—be conducted on an ambulatory basis. The author has had success with individual high-frequency supportive counseling during this phase of treatment. The main therapeutic emphasis during the frequent contacts (three one-hour sessions per week) has been on counseling only for present and future behavior.

In contrast, some escapist abusers have more frequently presented psychotic-like reactions to their interactions and activities. As opposed to the "uncovering" techniques utilized with adaptive abusers, a "covering" frame of reference has proven to be effective with such escapist abusers.

In summary, during this abstinent phase of treatment, the patient should receive frequent supportive sessions as he explores his intrapersonal and interpersonal capacities without the use of drugs. The ambulatory situation, with frequent therapeutic contact, seems best suited for this exploration, which will probably occupy several months. The long-term aftercare phase of treatment would appear to be managed most appropriately in regular, but somewhat less frequent group sessions. Indices of anxiety or depression, e.g. inappropriate changes in mood or affect, inability to cope with stress, any of which may signal a relapse episode, seem to be more readily detected. In addition to early detection, concentrated support and guidance are more available in group therapy settings. It has been our experience that reality therapy techniques may be most appropriate during this "continuous care" period.[26]

Hallucinogen Abusers

LSD is not physically addicting in the sense of barbiturates and opiates. The dependence is psychological, not physical. Tolerance develops rapidly after a few days of repeated use, but is usually lost in two or three days. Cross-tolerance exists among LSD, psilocybin, and mescaline, though tolerance to mescaline develops more slowly than to the other two. Paradoxically, some users report a state of increased sensitivity to LSD once they have lost their tolerance. Unexpected return of the drugged state without ingestion of LSD for months or even a year later has been reported.

The literature reports three different kinds of experiences under LSD: (1) *the good trip*—a predominantly pleasant experience; (2) *the bad trip*—a dysphoric experience characterized by anxiety, panic, feelings of persecution, fears of loss of ego boundaries, loss of control and time perception, and impaired performance; and (3) an *ambivalent state* where the subject may simultaneously experience contrasting feelings as of happiness and lightness, relaxedness, and tenseness.[26]

The *bad trip* has been well-documented in the literature. Becker described these as psychological and attributable to the panic emergency upon experiencing a host of overwhelming sensory inputs. Learning was entailed and described in relation to marijuana use. Frosch reported that, in a two and one half year period, some 250 persons were admitted to Bellevue with mental disorders either directly attributable to LSD or to the extent that the drug played a major role in bringing about the disorder. Patients admitted remained from a few days to several months, and a few were transferred to state hospitals.[39]

The acute reactions—the bad trips—are of two types:

1. *Psychotoxic reactions* are characterized by confusion and/or acute paranoia, feelings of omnipotence and invulnerability, which may cause the user to expose himself to dangers resulting, at times, in injury or death.

2. *Panic reactions* occur as a secondary response to the drug-induced symptoms.

One may anticipate fairly rapid recovery from these two acute states. Remission usually occurs within two or three days with the recommended treatment of sedation and verbal support.

Significant variables determining the course of any LSD trip are the personality and expectations of the subject, the presence of a dependable guide, the nature of the setting in which the drug is taken, and, according to Ungerleider and Freedman, the age of the subject. Younger subjects were noted to have experienced acute reactions more frequently.

For the acutely intoxicated state, the American Medical Association recommends the LSD abuser have an immediate trial with phenothiazine medication, preferably administered intramuscularly, since the phenothiazines block the action of LSD. They further suggest barbiturates can be used in lieu of, or in addition to phenothiazines. Because the hallucinogens do not cause physical dependence, there are no physical complications of withdrawal. Care should be exercised, however, to learn whether other addicting drugs were taken concurrently with the

LSD, which may require a separate detoxification regimen. Once the acute reaction or panic has subsided, sedatives or tranquilizers have been recommended.[39]

Suggested Treatment Modalities for Young Non-opiate Abusers

As mentioned already, very little thought has been given to developing suitable treatment modalities for the non-opiate abusers in view of our primary preoccupation with heroin addiction alone. It is most important that we begin to think through such approaches to deal with this problem as well as that of younger heroin users. What kind of facilities do we need and how should our existing techniques, developed for heroin users, be modified? The following section will outline some possibilities in this area.

In-patient Services and Detox Facilities

In-patient services and detox facilities are essential for: drug abusers who have become addicted to the barbiturates and some of the newer drugs such as Doriden, which require in-patient detoxification; heavy amphetamine users; "freakouts" on LSD and other drugs; the "new breed" of multiple drug abusers with, at times, multiple addictions; and persons whose psychological and social problems dictate a hospital stay removed from the community. This service will be a focal point for reaching and engaging young drug users in treatment.

Special Day Centers for Young Non-opiate Abusers

Youngsters more heavily involved in multiple drug use beyond the stage of initial exploration could be benefited by day centers with a variety of reinforcements built in. These could include the use of chemotherapy—either the narcotics antagonists, cyclazocine, naloxone, or low-dose methadone if they are primarily involved with the opiates; the use of civil commitment to hold them in treatment; probation in the sense of "rational authority"; and others. These youngsters would benefit from not being mixed with chronic users, and their special needs should be studied. The day center entails a considerable commitment on the part of the participants, since they will come in daily and spend most of the day there for therapy, training, recreation and education.

Specialized Non-opiate Residential Centers

Specialized non-opiate residential centers would be helpful to younger abusers who cannot function in the community and require a period of socialized living away from home. The special needs of this group would be studied, with emphasis on modification of existing techniques such as use of abrasive encounter and group therapy approaches, ex-heroin-addict role models, the involvement of family, special educational and vocational inputs, and others.

Outpatient Center

These centers will follow the model of some of the "Encounter" and "Span" centers located in New York City which formerly operated in close conjunction with residential centers such as "Phoenix" and "Daytop Lodge." They entail a considerably smaller investment of time than the day centers described in this section. Young drug abusers may come in from one to several times weekly to participate in encounter groups and other counseling to be weaned away from drugs. The center also serves as a screening point for referral to residential centers or other more intensive treatment if youngsters cannot make it on an ambulatory basis.

Similar Specialized Facilities for Adult Non-opiate Abusers Will Also Need to Be Developed

EDUCATION AND PREVENTION. Finally, we shall need to develop more effective educational and preventive approaches, with evaluation built in, to head off the drift to drug use; and, where indicated, reorient value systems towards more conventional modes of behavior. Our educational and preventive efforts to date have, regrettably, failed to reorient attitudes and emotional or other predispositions appreciably; we need to learn how to enhance our efforts in these areas. Emphasis will be placed on the use of peer-group counter-cultures to reinforce the preventive efforts. Role models would be users who had been involved with non-opiate abuse and perhaps more limited heroin use, but who broke away, rather than the conventional heroin ex-addict role model. The development of viable alternatives for living would be an important dimension, buttressed by the knowledge that drug use is dysfunctional and maladaptive for most users in the long run. Conventional pedantic methods of education may need to give away to more dynamic learning within the context of group processes geared to improve communication and enhance the understanding of interpersonal interactions, the special needs of youth, the disadvantaged, and other target populations of concern.

REFERENCES

1. Chein, I.; Lee, D. L., and Rosenfeld, E.: *The Road to H*. Basic Books, New York, 1964.
2. Brotman, R., and Freedman, A.: *A Community Health Approach to Drug Addiction*. Washington, U.S. Department of Health, Education and Welfare, J.D. Publication, No. 9005, 1968.
3. Merton, R. K.: *Social Theory and Social Structure*, revised ed. Free Press, New York, 1960.
4. Cloward, R., and Ohlin, L.: *Delinquency and Opportunity: A Theory of Delinquent Gangs*. Free Press, Glencoe, 1960.
5. Lindesmith, A.: *Opiate Addiction*. Principia, Evanston, 1947.
6. Brill, L.; Nash, G., and Langrod, J.: The dynamics of de-addiction. In Brill, L., and Lieberman, L.: *Major Modalities In the Treatment of Drug Abuse*. Behavioral Publications, New York, 1972.
7. Langrod, J., and Brill, L.: Special study of 119 methadone patients at Harlem Hospital. Study for Columbia Bureau of Applied Social Research, Mimeographed version, 1969.
8. Dole, V., and Nyswander, M.: Methadone-maintenance and its implications for theories of narcotics addiction. Presented at the 46th Annual Meeting of the Association for Research in Nervous and Mental Diseases, New York, December 3, 1968.
9. Alksne, H.; Lieberman, L., and Brill, L.: A conceptual model of the life cycle of addiction. *International Journal of the Addictions*, 2(2):221-240, Fall, 1967.
10. Martin, W. R., and Jasinski, D.: Physiological parameters of morphine dependence in man—tolerance, early abstinence, protracted abstinence. *J Psychiat Res*, 7:9-17, 1969.
11. Jaffe, J., and Brill, L.: Cyclazocine, a long-acting narcotic antagonist: Its voluntary acceptance as a treatment modality by narcotics abusers. *International Journal of the Addictions*, 1:99-123, January, 1966.
12. Brill, L., and Laskowitz, D.: Cyclazocine in the treatment of narcotics addiction—another look. Chapter in Proceedings, Eastern Psychiatric Research Association, 15th Annual Meeting, New York City, November 8, 1970.
13. Brill, L., and Jaffe, J.: The relevancy of some newer American treatment approaches for England. *Br J Addict*, 62:375-386, 1967.
14. Wikler, A.: Conditioning factors in opiate addiction and relapse. In

Wilner, D. M., and Kassebaum, G. G.: *Narcotics.* McGraw-Hill, New York, 1965.

15. O'Donnell, J. A.: Research problems in follow-up studies of addicts. In *Rehabilitating the Narcotics Addicts.* Washington, D.C., U.S. Government Printing Office, 1966.

16. Winick, C.: Maturing out of narcotic addiction. *Bulletin on Narcotics,* Vol. XIV, No. 1, January-March, 1962.

17. Duvall, H. J.; Locke, B., and Brill, L.: Follow-up study of narcotic addicts five years after hospitalization. *Public Health Rep,* 73:185-193, 1963.

18. Robbins, L. N., and Murphy, G. I.: Drug use in a normal population of young Negro men. *Am J Public Health,* 67:1580, 1967.

19. Jaffe, J.; Laskowitz, D., and Brill, L.: Cyclazocine intervention in the treatment of narcotics addiction. *The Bulletin,* N.Y.S. District Branch, American Psychiatric Association, Vol. X, No. 5, pp. 8-9, January, 1967.

20. Martin, W. R., and Sloan, J.: The pathophysiology of morphine dependence and its treatment with opioid antagonists. *Pharmako-psychiatrie Neuro-Psychopharmakologie,* Vol. 1, 1968.

21. Brill, L.: *Drug addiction. Encyclopedia of Social Work,* N.A.S.W., July, 1971.

22. Vaillant, G. E.: A twelve-year follow-up of New York narcotic addicts: II. The natural history of a chronic disease. *N Engl J Med,* 275(23):1282-1288, 1966.

23. Miller, W. B.: Lower-class culture as a generating milieu of gang delinquency. *Journal of Social Issues,* 14(No. 4), 1958.

24. Brill, L., and Lieberman, L.: *Major Modalities in the Treatment of Drug Abuse.* Behavioral Publications, New York, 1972.

25. Brill, L., and Chambers, C. D.: A multimodality approach to methadone treatment. *Social Work,* 16(No. 3), July, 1971.

26. Chambers, C. D., and Brill, L.: Some considerations in the treatment of non-narcotic drug abuse. N.Y.S. N.A.C.C. Reprint, New York, 1971. Also *Industrial Medicine and Surgery,* January, 1971.

27. Brill, L.; Chambers, C. D., and Inciardi, J.: Pentazocine (Talwin): Evidence of abuse potential. *Medical Counterpoint,* 3(No. 6), June, 1971.

28. Chambers, C. D.: An Assessment of Drug Use in the General Population. Special Report #1. *Drug Use in N.Y.S.* N.Y.S. N.A.C.C., May, 1971.

29. DeRopp, R. S.: *Drugs and the Mind.* Grove, New York, 1957.

30. Brill, L., and Lieberman, L.: *Authority and Addiction.* Little, Brown, Boston, 1969.

31. Brill, L.: Some comments on the paper "Social control in therapeutic communities" by Dan Waldorf. *International Journal of the Addictions,* 6(1):5-50, March, 1971.

32. Brill, L.: Three approaches to the casework treatment of narcotic addicts. *Social Work, 13*(No. 2), April, 1968.
33. Glasscote, R.; Jaffe, J. H.; Sussex, J.; Ball, J., and Brill, L.: The Treatment of Drug Abuse. A.P.A.-N.A.M.H. Publication, 1972.
34. Martin, W. R.; Gorodetsky, C. W., and McClare, T. R.: A proposed method for ambulatory treatment of narcotic addicts using a long-active orally effective narcotic antagonist, Cyclazocine. An experimental study. Comm. on Problems of Drug Dependence, 27th Meeting of the Nat. Academy of Science, Nat. Res. Council, Houston, Texas, Feb., 1967.
35. Chambers, C. D., and Brill, L.: Methadone: Issues and Experiences. Behavioral Publications, New York, 1972.
36. Chambers, C. D., and Taylor, W. J. R.: The incidence and patterns of drug abuse among long-term methadone maintenance patients. 33rd Annual Meeting, Committee on Problems of Drug Dependence, Nat. Res. Council, Nat. Acad. of Science, Toronto, Canada, Feb. 16-17, 1971.
37. Essig, C. F.: Addiction to barbiturate and non-barbiturate sedative drugs. In *Association for Research in Nervous and Mental Diseases: The Addictive States.* Williams and Wilkins, Baltimore, 1968.
38. Isbell, H., and Fraser, H.: Addiction to analgesics and barbiturates, Part II. *J Pharmacol Exp Ther, 99*(4):355-397, 1950.
39. Frosch, W. A.: Untoward reactions to LSD resulting in hospitalization. *N Engl J Med, 233*:1235-1239, 1965.

Appendix

THE "PUSHES AND PULLS" OF ADDICTION

1. No one factor is entailed in either starting or stopping drug use. Multi-causation and overdetermination of drug behavior.

2. Adaptive uses of drugs initially. Increasing maladaptiveness of drug life as time goes on. The drug use itself is necessary and wonderful, but the concomitant life style, punishments, and stresses become increasingly intolerable.

3. In the initial "honeymoon" period, for the working class, it may be an illegitimate means for achievement and status—as through selling.

"PUSHES"—PRESSURES FOR GETTING OFF

1. The bad life, arrests and prison, repeated hospitalizations for withdrawal and illness.

2. Negative self-image—need to cut off square associations, steal or prostitute, lose respective trappings—good clothing, nice "pad," money.

3. Dramatic happenings—narrow escapes, arrests, constant battles with square world, police, family, rehab personnel. O.D.'s and illness; need to be constantly on the move to get money for drugs and avoid withdrawal symptoms.

4. Exhaustion of resources—personal, psychological and material. Exhaustion of outside resources and supplies in form of family, friends, and other addicts.

5. Fading of glamour—recession of honeymoon phase, slave to habit and drug life, inability to get off the merry-go-round. Increasing punishments and battering down as time goes on. Realization must lose with drugs. Exhaustion, desperation, seeking for a way out.

"PULLS"–DRAW OF LEGITIMATE GOALS AND
CONVENTIONAL STANDARDS

1. Pull of legitimate aspirations which were never lost sight of–Two worlds in conflict–square and junkie.

2. Treatment facilities–existence of facilities which can help you get off drugs.

3. Personal relationships–this can be important–as in need to test love of mother and father; or in the event a new relationship is formed, though the latter proved very infrequent and addicts were better able to form constructive relationships only after completing treatment.

4. Opportunity to think, reflect–periods in jail or hospital did serve to help addicts take stock and examine what was happening to them.

5. Other factors were the length of drug history which becomes maladaptive in time. In this respect, we can think of a "maturing out;" in the sense, however, that addicts are ground down and are ready to consider other possibilities for living. In retrospect, they see themselves as "zombies," "living deaths," and "insane" and wonder how they could have lived this way for so many years. We can't always wait for addicts to "mature out," and many do not, especially if they are coping successfully with the drug life. Effective treatment approaches can short-circuit the process and rehabilitate addicts even if they haven't gone the whole circuit and are still very young–as our case studies revealed.

INDEX